BEYOND SCIENCE

DENIS ALEXANDER

Beyond Science

A. J. HOLMAN COMPANY
Division of J. B. Lippincott Company
Philadelphia and New York

U.S. Library of Congress Cataloging in Publication Data

Alexander, Denis.
    Beyond science.

        Bibliography: p.
        1. Civilization, Modern—1950–
        2. Science and civilization.   I. Title.
    CB430.A43   1973   901.94'7   72–10371
    ISBN-0-87981-017-3

CONTENTS

PREFACE

Why is it that so many are turning away from science? What is the basis for this reaction which has gained such impetus during the past ten years?

Certainly some are frightened at the implications of current research. Others have been sickened by the applications of science in modern warfare. Many are finding that science is not fulfilling the role that has been given it: it has been made a god but has been found wanting; the world-view of its proponents is too narrow – man is losing his humanity in a technological society.

At the same time the very rationalism underlying the methods of science is under attack. There is a drift towards non-rational or deliberately anti-rational ways of thinking. Many believe that it is necessary to deny man's reason in order to restore his humanity through the way of mystical experience.

Is there an answer to this dilemma? Has man's reason created powers which are beyond his control? What is the way forward? Various answers are being proposed. But do they fit the facts? The aim of this book is to look not only at the reasons for the reaction against science, but to examine some of the answers. In grappling with the depths of the problems involved, and the nature of man himself who has created them, one answer seems to stand out from the others as one which makes sense of the evidence available. It is to this answer that an increasing number of people, especially younger people, are turning today. It is with the validity and implications of this answer that this book is concerned.

Chapter One
SCIENCE IN THE SEVENTIES

At a meeting of the American Association for the Advancement of Science which met at Chicago in December 1970, Dr Edward Teller, father of the H-bomb, fearing physical attack, arranged to be protected by five armed bodyguards. Anti-war demonstrators presented him with a trophy 'in recognition of his services in the cause of war'. It showed a policeman firing a pistol with the inscription 'I am just following orders'. Dr Glenn Seaborg, chairman of the Atomic Energy Commission, fled the lecture-room rather than hear himself indicted by hecklers for the crime of 'science against the people'. Dr Teller remarked that 'Science is a sacred word to me, but there are those who want to make it into a political circus'.

It is interesting to trace the evolution of a scientific theory from when it was first put forward to this kind of opposition and social impact.

In 1905 Einstein's equation $E = mc^2$ was published, showing that mass could be converted into energy. Scientists doubted whether it was technically feasible. But, according to their knowledge, it was a possibility.

At 5.30 a.m. on Monday 16 July 1945, the possibility became a reality. A mushroom cloud billowed up over the desert at Alamogordo, New Mexico, with complete devastation inside a one-mile diameter.

On 6 August 1945, Hiroshima. On 9 August, Nagasaki.

After the war the physicist Heisenberg reported that, in the summer of 1939, 'Twelve people might still have been able, by coming to mutual agreement, to prevent the construction of atom bombs.'

9

In the 1950s there was continuous opposition to the construction of nuclear weapons. Talks broke down. The first H-bomb was exploded on Elugelab, a coral island, on 1 November 1952. At its site is a crater 175 feet deep and one mile long.

During the 1960s a partial ban on nuclear tests was negotiated. The authority set up in Vienna to police the agreement found it impossible to apply the ban effectively. As weapons became increasingly sophisticated there was increasing hope that no one would be mad enough to use them for war. At the same time there was increasing disillusionment with the efforts of science and technology. Vietnam highlighted the fact that science had made large-scale cruelty incomparably easier. In the US a group of scientists did research to find how to make napalm stick more closely to human flesh. It was reported that by the end of 1969 in Vietnam more than $5\frac{1}{2}$ million acres of forest and cropland had been sprayed with herbicides, destroying one-half of the mangrove forests and one-fifth of the hardwood forests. There was increasing international concern about pollution. There was a shift away from science in secondary schools. There was a worldwide ferment amongst students characterized by a reaction against the machine-like grip of society on university life. There was a growing desire by society to control the decisions of a scientific-technological élite.

All this and much more lies behind the 'political circus' at Chicago in 1970. The road from sophisticated theory through research and technological development to human application and full social impact is a long one. Long-term effects are extremely difficult to predict.

Where are we going in the 1970s? One-fifth of the world scientific manpower is still employed for military purposes. Yet deeper than such sobering facts are the nagging questions about the whole role of science in society. In Britain probably less than one in four scientists have complete freedom to publish their results. About 60 per cent are employed in industry, where they are restricted by commercial security, and about 20 per cent are employed by the government. Often society does not even know what the scientist is doing, let alone have the ability to control it.

An encouraging move in many countries has been the recent formation of groups to arouse a social conscience amongst scientists and raise up a body of informed public opinion. The British Society for Social Responsibility in Science is a definite step in the right direction. In fact it is now quite fashionable for scientists to have a social conscience. One hopes the fashion will not prove to be a passing one.

But the national control of scientific application in technology is relatively easy compared with the thorny problem of international control. One cannot avoid the niggling doubt that whilst world policies are directed by political expediency, one single misuse of science anywhere is likely to have its own special repercussions. If another country is going to attack you with biological weapons, then you need to know how to defend yourself. And to defend yourself you need to know how they work. And to know how they work you need to make them. And if you know how to make them, even if you do not stockpile them, you could always make more if you wanted to. The circle is a vicious one.

One of the outstanding features of the past twenty-five years of scientific research has been the fundamental advances made in the biological sciences. This 'biological revolution' has often been likened to the discoveries in physics which dominated the scientific world earlier this century. Few, as we have already remarked, could have predicted the long-term results of these discoveries. But there have been no lack of those with forebodings about our increasing understanding of the mechanisms of life itself.

When Aldous Huxley wrote *Brave New World* in 1931, the world of soma and blood surrogate seemed remote. Drug-users were a small minority. The science of molecular biology was in its infancy. The possibility of synthesizing life artificially seemed very far away.

Yet in 1958, a few years before his death from cancer, Huxley wrote: 'When *Brave New World* was being written, I was convinced that there was still plenty of time . . . these things were coming all right, but not in my time, not even in the time of my grandchildren.' Then he adds: 'The prophecies . . . are coming true much sooner than I thought they would.'

In the 1970s many molecular biologists are facing a crisis of conscience equivalent to that faced by nuclear physicists after the atom bomb. Matthew Meselson, the Harvard biologist, has warned of the 'revolution in biochemistry and molecular biology, leading to the most detailed and subtle knowledge of the living process' which 'inevitably will allow man to manipulate and control living things, including himself in ways that cannot now be spelled out . . .'

Recently a spate of books have been published with titles such as *The Biological Time-Bomb*, *The Doomsday Book*, *The Science of War and Peace* and even the exotic *How to be a Survivor: A Plan to Save Spaceship Earth*. The message of these books is gloomy but plain. By the turn of the century the world population will be around 7,000 million. Countries such as Brazil and Indonesia will be roughly comparable in size of population with the US and Soviet Union. Increasing population density will lead to increasing pollution. Deaths due to war are going up by a steady progression. Large-scale famines are likely in the 1980s. Furthermore the applications of present-day biological discovery to everyday life are liable to make even the results of the advent of nuclear power pale in comparison.

Is this an over-dramatisation? 'Was God throwing dice when he made the universe?' asks Jacques Monod in *Chance and Necessity*. Certainly basic questions are involved. Or is it just to cash in on the present trend towards pessimism? Undoubtedly gloom about the future is now fashionable, just as optimism was in fashion at the turn of the century. In reporting biological discoveries there is a special danger of exaggeration, often because they are misunderstood. In fact the mass media seem obsessed by the bizarre. The slightest advance in assembling a living cell from its constituents may be guaranteed to produce screaming head-lines of 'test-tube babies'. The merest hint of being able to help memory retention may well make a rapid evolution in the press to 'miracle memory pill'. It is often difficult to get at the real facts.

Let us therefore take a sober look at two branches of biological science, genetics and brain science, which are liable to take some more big steps forward during the 1970s. What are their potentialities for the good of mankind? How could they be misused? Those who object even to over-simplified technicalities may prefer to pass over the paragraphs which follow. But the aim in being factual and descriptive is to avoid sensationalism on the one hand and under-estimation of what is at stake on the other.

Genes, sex and society

All the information for our inheritance, from blue eyes to knobbly knees, is embodied in a nucleic acid called DNA. This consists of two strands of chemical units, called nucleotides, which are wound round each other rather like intertwined coiled springs. There are four kinds of nucleotides. These are the 'letters' of the 'genetic alphabet'. It is the specific order of these four nucleotides in the strand which determines the genetic information. Each nucleotide on one strand pairs exactly with its 'opposite number' on the other strand. It is this pairing which holds the two strands together.

Now proteins, which are the basic building materials of living matter, consist of chains of amino-acids. One protein may contain several chains locked together. The three-dimensional structures of many proteins are now known very precisely. About ten new protein structures are being published every year. The structure of the protein is controlled by the sequence of the amino-acids. Twenty different amino-acids are found in the proteins present in man. The alteration of only one amino-acid in the sequence may profoundly alter the structure of the protein. Enzymes are simply the proteins which catalyse living processes.

The gene is that length of DNA strand which codes for one protein, or sometimes one amino-acid chain of the protein. The genetic code was cracked during the 1960s, and it is known that each amino-acid is coded for by three nucleotides in the genetic alphabet. A protein consisting of a chain of 100 amino-acids would therefore be coded by a gene at least 300 nucleotides long, since 'stop' and 'go' signals are also included in the code.

Mistakes which arise in the genes are called mutations. These may arise in various ways. For instance, when the DNA replicates itself (by a process not yet fully understood) the copying may not be perfect, leading to a mistake in the new DNA. Or by chemical or radioactive means one of the nucleotides may be damaged.

Andthecat

makes sense if you know that all the words in the phrase are of three letters. But

ndt hec at

which is nonsense may well be the result if the 'a' is damaged. A gene's message may similarly be turned to nonsense if only one nucleotide is damaged.

In certain mutations the change is so slight that it results in one amino-acid in a long protein chain being exchanged for another one. Yet this might alter the properties of the protein considerably. For instance haemoglobin is the protein in the blood which carries the oxygen we breathe to the body's tissues. It consists of four chains of amino-acids locked together. There is a variant of this protein called Haemoglobin Hiroshima, so called because of its discovery in a Japanese family. In 1971 Professor Max Perutz, working in Cambridge, showed that the abnormality was due to the substitution of the 146th amino-acid in one of the chains with another amino-acid. This single minute change is enough to alter completely the properties of the haemoglobin.

When the DNA molecule replicates itself, it makes a 'mirror-image' copy of each of its two strands of nucleotides. The result is two identical daughter DNA molecules. Any mistakes may thus be communicated to the progeny.

Fortunately DNA is very stable, and mutations occurring in the germ cells, which will therefore be passed on to the children, are very rare. This is just as well, since mutations are almost always harmful. Experiments suggest that one germ cell in 100,000, or perhaps only one in a million, carries a recent mutation. When mutations take place in cells other than germ cells, a cancerous tumour may result, but of course this will not be passed on to the children.

That DNA is very stable may be seen by studying various family trees. The protruding and rather ugly lip which characterized the Hapsburg royal family is a good example. This is probably the work of just one dominant gene. Fortunately those who painted the Hapsburg family did not play down this particular deformity so it can be traced through to modern times. Some possessors of the lip were the Emperor Maximilian I (born in the fifteenth century), the Emperor Charles V (sixteenth century), Maria Theresa of Austria and Archduke Charles of Teschen (eighteenth century) and Alfonso XII of Spain (nineteenth century).

Since DNA is so stable it means that mistakes will persist for many generations. However in each cell we have two copies of each chromosome. The chromosomes are the bodies which carry the genetic information and consist of groups of DNA molecules held together by protein. This means that every cell normally has two good copies of all the genetic information needed for its various characteristics. When there is only one defective gene it is the good 'dominant' gene which is normally followed. In this case the bad gene is known as 'recessive', and its wrong information is not expressed. The results of damaged DNA will therefore only be seen in cases where two recessives are present in the same cell.

The word 'dominant' may in fact be applied to any gene whose information is expressed in preference to that of another gene coding for the same organ or function. For instance the brown-eye gene is dominant to the blue. Babies may have inherited from their parents either brown and brown, brown and blue, blue and brown, or blue and blue genes. In the first three cases the baby's eyes will be brown, and only in the last will they be blue.

We now know that about four per cent of all babies are born with some kind of genetic defect. About one half of all cases of congenital blindness, and about one half of all cases of congenital deafness, are genetically determined by mutant genes, mostly recessive. Genetic factors are extensively involved in certain cases of heart disease. About one third of all instances of severe mental retardation are due to the extra 'G' chromosome which is responsible for Mongolism. More than 130 genetic defects are known which affect mental ability. These are listed in McKusick's *Mendelian Inheritance in Man*. Some of these defects have been observed in only a very few cases. Perhaps the best known is the disease phenylketonuria, where the DNA strand which codes for the enzyme which converts the amino-acid phenylalanine to tyrosine is either defective or missing. Unless detected, formation from phenylalanine of harmful side-products may cause permanent brain damage.

Other malformations clearly have very complex causes, but there are indications that some, such as spina bifida, a disease of the spinal cord, have a genetic component. A genetic factor has been implicated in schizophrenia, though its exact implication in the disease remains controversial.

Some genetic defects are linked with the chromosomes that determine sex. Each normal human cell contains 23 pairs of chromosomes. One of these 23 pairs determines the sex. In the female there are two X chromosomes, and in the male one X and one Y chromosome, and the male sperm is a 50–50 mixture of cells containing X and Y chromosomes. Whether the ovum is fertilized by a sperm containing an X chromosome or a Y chromosome will therefore determine whether the child will be a boy or a girl.

If the sex chromosomes cause a person's sex, they also possess genes which cause characteristics irrelevant to sex, such as colour-blindness, webbed toes, muscular dystrophy and a disease called haemophilia. In haemophilia there is a defective blood-clotting mechanism. This is due to a defective recessive gene attached to the X chromosome. A man receives his X chromosome from his mother, never from his father. On 7 April 1853, assisted by the new gas chloroform, Queen Victoria gave birth to her eighth child. Little Prince Leopold turned out to be a 'bleeder', and eventually died from a fall at the age of 31. This was the first indication that Queen Victoria was a carrier of haemophilia, and with time this mutant gene was spread through her descendants to many royal houses of Europe.

What chances are there of preventing these inherited genetic abnormalities? In bacteria genetic engineering is already a reality. New genetic material may be introduced by means of viruses. But here the situation is relatively simple. In many bacteria there is only a single strand of DNA. However in man the situation is vastly more complicated. In a single human germ cell there are 46 chromosomes. The number of nucleotide pairs in the DNA distributed amongst those chromosomes is in the order of 1,000 million. Many of the genes are responsible for producing 'repressors' which 'switch off' other genes. Therefore an alteration in only one gene may have widespread effects in many other genes scattered over several different chromosomes. Furthermore the information for a structural protein, or the pattern of a nerve network or a complex series of chemical reactions, may well be coded for by complex sets of genes again spread over many different chromosomes.

Of course genetic counselling is already a reality. Couples both carrying defective recessive genes may be advised against having children. It is also now possible, without injury to mother or child, to obtain cells of foetal origin, but not part of the foetus. If examination of the chromosomes shows certain deviations, it may be predicted with assurance that the foetus will develop into a grossly abnormal child. The parents are then faced with the difficult choice of whether or not the mother should have an abortion.

Yet all this is very far from direct tampering with the genes themselves. That this may one day be a reality is suggested by several lines of research currently in progress.

In 1969 Dr R. G. Edwards, working at Cambridge, reported the first fertilization of the human ovum carried out under laboratory conditions. Until recently studies in human conception were very limited, mainly because of the inaccessibility of the ovary. It was difficult therefore to obtain oocytes, those cells which have not developed into mature ova. The breakthrough came with the discovery that human oocytes would undergo their final stages of development, those occurring just before ovulation, when removed from their storage follicles in the body and placed in a suitable culture medium. It is human oocytes thus matured which were first artificially fertilized.

The growth of the fertilized ovum to the blastocyst stage, the stage at which there are about one hundred cells present in the embryo, was reported in 1971, both by Dr Edwards and by Dr Landrum Shettles working in New York. The blastocyst stage is reached 5–6 days after ovulation, and is the stage at which the embryo is planted into the wall of the womb. Work is currently in progress to find ways of re-implanting human embryos into the womb which have been grown artificially in the laboratory. Once this has been accomplished, and it may be accomplished very soon, there will be several immediate social consequences. One will be the cure of certain types of infertility, particularly where the wife has a blocked oviduct or the husband produces only a small number of effective sperm, mixed with many malformed ones.

Another development may well be the determination of the sex of the embryo before transfer to the womb, but this awaits the arrival of a method which could clearly identify enzyme activity or antigens which are linked to genes which determine sex. Once the sex of the blastocyst could be determined then the way would be opened to control sex-linked mutant genes in men by avoiding the birth of affected boys. This would not mean the elimination of the faulty gene. It would simply mean that the gene was passed on to the daughters, and they too would have to undergo the same process of having several blastocysts checked for sex in the laboratory before having children by re-implantation of a female blastocyst into the womb.

Another way in which sex could be determined is based on the small weight difference which exists between sperm containing the Y (male) chromosome and those containing the X (female) chromosome. However, attempts to separate the two types of sperm, based on this difference in weight, have not so far met with complete success.

Dr Anne McLaren, the Edinburgh geneticist, has suggested that the ability to choose the sex of one's children could be routinely possible within the next thirty years, and would have the immediate effect of lowering the birth rate. Surveys in Britain have shown that most people want a two-child family, one boy and one girl. Surveys have also shown that there is a slight preference for having a boy rather than a girl. A close control would therefore be necessary to avoid an uneven sex ratio in the population. Of course in certain cultures where the preference for a boy is extremely high, control would be very much more difficult.

It should be emphasized that the growth of an embryo to a recognizable human foetus under laboratory conditions is still a very long way in the future. So far the growth achieved under artificial conditions represents only a little more than four per cent of the total period of development between fertilization of the ovum and birth of the baby. However the difficulties to be overcome, though great, are purely technical ones. Several groups of scientists are engaged in the development of an artificial placenta, with the immediate aim of preserving the life of prematurely born babies. Animal embryos have already been kept alive for considerable periods under laboratory conditions. Dr Yu-Chih Hsu working at the John Hopkins University in the USA has developed a technique for growing mouse embryos in the laboratory well beyond the blastocyst stage until the beginnings of heart-beat can be observed. Some embryos have been cultivated for two weeks. The possibility of begetting babies artificially is well out of the science-fiction class and into the bounds of technical possibility.

Dr Max Perutz, Nobel prize-winner and one of Britain's leading scientists, has been amongst those who have attacked research in this field. He has claimed that Dr Edwards' aim to fertilize ova in the test-tube and re-implant these ova into infertile women is 'absolute madness'. 'Even if only a single abnormal baby is born and has to be kept alive as an invalid for the rest of its life Dr Edwards would have a terrible guilt upon his shoulders.' Dr Perutz suggests that the results of such experiments could have 'horrifying' results similar in proportion to the thalidomide tragedy.

It has recently been shown that every cell of the body, however specialized, contains the same amount of genetic information. In other words, a brain cell contains all the information needed to be a cell in the intestines, but the relevant genes have been 'switched off' in a way not yet fully understood. Equally an intestine cell has the potential to be a brain cell.

This has been shown experimentally by Dr J. B. Gurdon working at Oxford. The nucleus of a mature frog's egg, that part of the cell which contains the chromosomes, was destroyed using a small beam of radiation. This was then replaced with a nucleus taken from the intestinal cell of the same frog. It was found that the egg developed normally into a tadpole, and then into a fully grown frog which could itself reproduce normally. All the information needed to make the eyes, brain, nose, legs, heart, liver, etc. of the new frog was coded in the DNA taken from that one fully developed intestinal cell. Furthermore the frog produced was identical to its one parent in every respect, since all the genetic information was received from a single source.

Until recently it was not possible to repeat this experiment in mammals, partly because mammalian eggs are so small – about one-hundredth of an inch across in the case of man. This technical difficulty has now been overcome by a group of scientists working at the Sloan-Kettering Institute for Cancer Research in New York. They have developed microsurgical techniques using high-powered microscopes and very fine needles whereby the chromo-somal material of single human cells may be manipulated. The possibility may therefore be opened up to remove the genetic material from the cells of, for example, a growing embryo in the laboratory, and place these in mature ova. If the fertilization of a whole series of identical ova was achieved under artificial conditions, and the blastocysts obtained were then implanted in different women, the result would be a series of identical children with the same genes. An alternative would be to use genetic material from the mother's own body and use it to fertilize artificially a series of her own ova. The result would then be not only a series of identical children, but children identical in every respect also to their own 'genetic mother'. This would be analogous to 'cloning', a process which is already possible in a wide variety of plants – the production of a genetically identical mass of cells from a single cell.

However abhorrent these kinds of possibilities might seem, they are a distinct possibility for the not-too-distant future. Clearly they would give the ability to breed large series of offspring from genetically outstanding parents. Some scientists and politicians have already suggested the establishment of an international board of control which would vet the ethics and longterm results of such experiments. But it is very unlikely that any world-wide control would be possible.

In contrast to these ways in which human cells could soon be manipulated, any direct interference with the human genetic material itself is at present out of the question. But various possibilities as to how control could be exerted are being considered. Some geneticists, perhaps too optimistically, believe that repair of specific genetic defects might well be possible in the next twenty or thirty years.

One possible technique could be a further development of experiments which have already been carried out. It has been shown that cells from other animals can be injected into a mouse embryo, and their multiplication during growth of the foetus can lead to the partial colonization of many organs. The foetus therefore grows into a 'chimaera', a mouse modified by the characteristics of the animal donor.

It seems that various body tissues of an adult each grow from their own small group of cells present in the foetus soon after fertilization. The various tissues which make up human blood, for instance, may be present in the embryo as fewer than six cells.

Clearly if a few cells were injected into the embryo at this critical stage of development, there could be the most profound effects. Benefits certainly include the masking of genetic defects present in the recipient, but the donated cells would also partially colonize brain and nervous tissue.

Selection of the appropriate donor cells could eventually be used to influence personal characteristics. Already newborn children suffering from deficiency diseases have been given donor cells capable of repairing the deficiency. Colonization during the earliest stages of development would obviously increase the chances of a close relationship between the donor cells and those of the receiving embryo. It should also be pointed out that if animal cells were used to colonize a human embryo, the result would be a man-animal chimaera.

Another possible technique for controlling genetic information has come from the work of Professor Henry Harris, of Oxford University. Professor Harris has used a virus to cause the formation of hybrid cells. For instance, a cell from a mouse and a human cell may be fused together to form a single cell with a 'double-quota' of genetic material. The fact that this new cell can continue to function and divide shows that there is nothing radically different between the DNA of the two cells. In one case two cells, each with a specific enzyme deficiency, have been joined to yield a hybrid cell containing both previously deficient enzymes. Each cell has therefore been used to 'cure' the other. Furthermore, it is now possible to eliminate chromosomes from the hybrids selectively, either those coming from the human or from the animal cells. This may eventually open up the way to 'tailoring' cells to have a certain genetic content.

Yet another possible technique for introducing new information into a cell could be by the introduction of virus-like particles containing DNA that can determine some particular biochemical function. This has now been carried out by a research group working in Bethesda, Maryland. Human cells from a patient suffering from galactosaemia, a rare disease in which the body cannot use the sugar galactose, were grown in the laboratory. A virus which normally infects bacteria was then used to transfer the 'good' gene from the bacteria to the human cells. The human cells were in this way 'cured' by using the bacterial enzyme needed to use the galactose. It may be some time before this technique could be applied to a living person, and there may always be the danger of damaging human genes already present. Also, if the operation was carried out at the level of the germ cell, it would be difficult to predict how many other effects might eventually appear in the whole individual.

Some of these difficulties might be overcome if the whole genetic information in a complete DNA strand could be programmed and transformed complete. Recently a complete bacterial gene (which was found to be biologically active) has been synthesized in the laboratory. Clearly this could open up the way to introducing specific information into new cells formed. However, we are far from finding out which genes in man code for which of his various characteristics, let alone synthesizing a human gene artificially. It has also been found possible to incorporate foreign DNA, for example DNA from mouse cells, into recipient cells from another animal which are being cultivated artificially in the laboratory. When the DNA in the receiving cells replicates, a small amount of the mouse DNA is incorporated into the DNA in the daughter cells. This could be another way of 'feeding' a cell with new genes.

Still further away, in the next century rather than in this, is the possibility of tinkering with our intelligence. Scientists will probably be arguing for a long time to come how much of our intelligence is inherited and how much is due to our environment. Professor Hans Eysenck believes that as much as 75 per cent of our intelligence is inherited. Whatever the correct percentage is finally found to be, it is clear that at least some intelligence quota must be built into the DNA code. It follows logically therefore that we may eventually be able to alter intelligence.

In many ways molecular biologists at present are in the position of physicists near the beginning of the century. Whilst the theoretical outlines are clear, the technical ability to make a human application, and therefore full social impact, are still in the future.

During the past twenty-five years we have found out the structure of the genetic material, DNA. We have cracked the genetic code. We have found out how the gene information is translated into protein structure. The basic outline of our inheritance is clear. During the 1970s dozens of research teams round the world are working on such problems as how DNA replicates itself, how genes are switched 'on' and 'off', how cells know how to turn into a liver rather than a kidney, and how genes could be altered artificially.

More research means more understanding of the life process itself and the mechanism of our inheritance. More understanding means more control. More control means more power. Happily this power may eventually mean the healing of thousands of genetically sick people, and the prevention of the birth of grossly abnormal children. But Professor Salvador Luria, one of the world's leading biologists, has spoken of a feeling 'not of optimism but one of tremendous fear' when he considers just how far this power could be misapplied. The geneticist Professor Nirenberg has emphasized that 'man may be able to programme his own cells with synthesized information long before he will be able to assess adequately the long-term consequences of such alterations, long before he will be able to formulate goals, and long before he can resolve the ethical and moral problems which will be raised.'

'Take care to be born well' advised Bernard Shaw. And it was J. B. S. Haldane who suggested that if the unscrupulous get rich and the poor have more children, at any rate we should expect some moral improvement! But what is 'well'? And what is 'moral'? What qualities in man are most desirable? Who is to say what is good for the future of man?

The French social philosopher Jacques Ellul has argued in the book *The Technological Society* that if the choice as to what type of human is desirable be left to those who are making the choice possible – the geneticists – then the doom of humanity must result. Why? Because the geneticists will make the new human in their own image. This proposition Ellul, not unreasonably, finds an unattractive one.

But who then is going to decide – the majority vote? When Hitler instituted a small programme of eugenics at Ordensburgen during the Second World War to encourage the breeding of children of Aryan appearance, was he right because the majority had elected him? How totally inadequate any kind of utilitarian ethic is to answer these questions we shall discuss in chapter four. Francis Crick has put it: 'The development of biology is going to destroy to some extent our traditional grounds for ethical beliefs, and it is not easy to see what to put in their place.'

Chemistry on the brain

Two handfuls of tissue, weighing a little more than 3lbs, with the colour and something of the consistency of porridge, are man's equipment for feeling, speaking, seeing, smelling, appreciating art, remembering, enjoying sex, doing cross-words, and all the hundred-and-one other activities that make up our daily lives.

The human brain contains about ten thousand million nerve cells. Each cell may connect with about ten thousand others. This means that if you could make a model of the brain using cells the size of a volume of the *Encyclopedia Britannica*, you would need nearly the whole of the earth's surface in which to lay it all out. In comparison to the brain's ten thousand million cells, the biggest computers yet built manage less than a hundred thousand units.

Brain research was initially the domain of neuro-physiologists – those particularly concerned with the electrical events involved. In a much-quoted description, Sir Charles Sherrington pictured the brain as 'an enchanted loom where millions of flashing shuttles weave a dissolving pattern'. However it was soon realized that the chemical events taking place in the brain were at least as important as the electrical events. Indeed the two are very closely linked. In the past thirty years a vast range of drugs have been discovered which affect the chemistry of the brain in remarkably different ways.

Many of these drugs may be extracted from plants and fungi which have been used by man for medical and religious purposes for thousands of years. Already by the nineteenth century trials were being carried out on drugs which affected human behaviour. One French doctor called Moreau de Tours published some results in 1845 on a drug called 'dawamesc'. Moreau had tried using 'dawamesc' to heal mental patients. The fact that it did not work very well was hardly surprising. 'Dawamesc' was what we now call cannabis.

In 1897 Arthur Heffter described his subjective experiences after ingestion of some peyote, or mescal cactus. He concluded that mescaline was the ingredient responsible for his heightened perception. The cactus had been used by Mexican Indians from time immemorial.

Two Swiss chemists called Stoll and Hofmann were working in 1938 on extracts from ergot, a fungus which grows on rye. It was rye bread infected with ergot which probably caused the outbreaks of Dancing Mania which first occurred in Aix-la-Chapelle in 1374 following the Black Death. From the fungus the two chemists were able to synthesize a new drug called LSD-25. Five years later Hofmann accidentally inhaled some LSD while carrying out drug trials. His resulting hallucinations caused him to carry out a controlled experiment a week later. A clear link was shown between LSD ingestion and the resulting vivid delusions and hallucinations.

However it was not until the early fifties that drugs such as LSD and mescaline began to receive much public attention. Aldous Huxley wrote in *The Doors of Perception* in 1954: '. . . one bright May morning I swallowed four tenths of a gramme of mescaline dissolved in half a glass of water and sat down to wait for the results . . .' Soon it became fashionable for journalists to take drugs and write books about their experiences. The LSD craze hit American universities in the 1960s.

The first drug which was to cause a major revolution in

psychiatry was chlorpromazine. This was first synthesized in 1950, and used in the therapy of a psychotic patient for the first time on 19 January 1952, at Val-de-Grâce, the famous military hospital in Paris. Three weeks later the patient was well, and was in fact discharged from hospital one week before the first article on chlorpromazine appeared in print. Within a few years the drug was being used worldwide to calm disturbed and psychotic patients. It soon became known under the French trade name Largactil, though it has numerous other names.

This discovery led to a boom in the search for drugs which would affect the mind. In fact extracts from the shrub *Rauwolfia serpentina* had long been known to have effects similar to chlor-promazine and were commonly used by Indian psychiatrists by 1950. In some parts of Asia *Rauwolfia* has the local name of 'pala-ka-dawa' which means 'insanity herb', an indication that its effects on the mind were well known by local natives. In 1947 the 'sedative principle' was extracted from the roots of the shrub, and in 1956 this active principle, called reserpine, was synthesized in the laboratory. Though the drug, in contrast to chlorpromazine, is now little used in psychiatry, it is still widely used in brain research.

By the late fifties a bewildering array of mind-affecting drugs had been discovered. Other hallucinogens were extracted. In 1958 Hofmann isolated psilocybin and psilocin from Mexican mush-rooms. In 1960 certain derivatives of LSD and other drugs were isolated by Hofmann from the Mexican *Rivea corymbosa* or 'Morning Glory', long used by the ancient Aztecs and modern Mexican Indians in experiencing hallucinations.

It is easy to become confused by such a vast range of mind-affecting drugs. We may divide them into roughly six groups.

The sedatives, or hypnotics, such as alcohol and the barbiturates, lower mental alertness and bodily activity, and induce sleep. It is estimated that about one night's sleep in every ten in Britain is hypnotic-induced, in other words produced by sleeping pills. There are 20 million prescriptions each year for barbiturates and 5 million for non-barbiturate hypnotics.

The stimulants, such as caffeine and the amphetamines, decrease fatigue and increase mental and physical activity.

The major tranquillizers, such as chlorpromazine and reserpine, are those which have a calming effect, particularly in reducing psychotic over-activity and excitement.

The minor tranquillizers are those used in calming anxiety and tension, but which do not produce the sedative effects of the barbiturates. An example is the drug meprobromate, which is sold under the trade-name Miltown.

The antidepressives include a wide range of drugs which produce euphoria, increase the amount of talking, speed reaction times, and generally act as stimulants. Their main value is in combating the severe depressions of mental patients. One of these drugs was discovered through an interest in the structure of chlorpromazine. A slight chemical modification of chlorpromazine produced imipramine, which was found to relieve depression, and which was then marketed as Tofranil. Another class of antidepressives are the MAO inhibiters. These are drugs which inhibit the mono-amine oxidases, enzymes which normally destroy excess transmitter substances in the brain. One example is isocarboxazid, more commonly known under its trade name of Marplan.

The last group of drugs are the hallucinogens such as LSD and mescaline. They are also known as the psychedelic, or literally mind-expanding drugs. An alternative name for drugs of this type is 'psychotomimetic', which means 'psychosis-imitating' or simply 'maddening'. The effects of these drugs are very well documented, and vary widely depending on the personality, current state of mind and environment of the person taking them. For instance one person who took one-fifth of a milligramme of LSD became psychotic, another taking the same dose claimed only that his eyes were blurred so that he found it harder to watch TV that evening. For most people only very small amounts of LSD are needed to produce hallucinations. One French journalist worked out the intriguing statistic that only 20 litres of LSD would be needed to send the whole US population on a trip for about six hours. Feelings of anguish, ecstasy and insight have all been produced by LSD, together with distortions of perception and a vast range of illusions. For some the 'acid trip' is heaven. For others it is hell. For some there is transcendental bliss, at least for a few hours. For others there are attempts to fly out of the window, with resulting death, or uncontrolled attacks on people around.

All of these drugs, except those of the last group, primarily affect mood. None of them has any effect on the information content of the brain. The psychedelic drugs normally have only temporary effects, though in some cases there are persistent or recurring hallucinations long after the drug has been discontinued.

During the seventies an enormous amount of research is being carried out into exactly how these various drugs affect brain mechanisms. Our knowledge is still very sketchy. No neat molecular system can be outlined as it can with our genetic inheritance. There are many hypotheses.

Several theories centre around transmitter substances. There is no direct electrical connection between the cells, or neurons as they are called, of nerve tissue. Instead the transmitting end of the neuron is connected by a sticky pad to another neuron. These junctions are called synapses. The actual connection is made by means of chemical transmitters which carry the 'electrical message' across the narrow gap which occurs in the synapse between one cell and the next. Some of these transmitters have the effect of stimulating the next cell, whilst some have an inhibitory effect. In fact it is just as well that there is inhibition in the brain. One writer has pictured the sensitivity of cerebral neurons as an enormous synaptic powder barrel which would explode in epileptic convulsions in the absence of inhibitory systems.

The transmitter substances are stored in 'packets' near the synaptic junctions. In peripheral nerves – that is nerves which are not part of the central nervous system which includes the brain and spinal cord – it is known that noradrenaline and acetylcholine are two of the transmitter substances. In the brain the situation is not so clear, though a wide range of substances such as serotonin, dopamine and GABA, as well as noradrenaline and acetylcholine, are all thought to be involved.

Mind drugs have a wide range of effects on these chemical transmitters. For instance reserpine reduces the amount of noradrenaline in the brain cells, whilst chlorpromazine blocks its release. The result is the same. Fewer impulses can flow between those nerve cells which use noradrenaline as their transmitter substance. The effect will be to 'calm down' certain nerve cells. This explains why such drugs do not in themselves 'cure' the mental illness. Instead they reduce the level of brain activity in a general way, so allowing the normal patterns of brain function to be restored.

By way of contrast amphetamine has the opposite effect to chlorpromazine. It stimulates the release of the transmitter from its storage 'packets' in the synapses and tends to block the process whereby noradrenaline is normally reabsorbed by the cells. Those cells using noradrenaline therefore become over-activated, resulting in the familiar mental over-excitement and alertness. People who have taken large continual doses of amphetamines often appear depressed. This may be due to the depletion of the noradrenaline stores. In other words the noradrenaline is being released by the amphetamines faster than it can be re-synthesized.

The ways in which psychedelic drugs exert their effect on the mind may be much more complicated. LSD is chemically very similar to serotonin, one of the chemical transmitters. It has therefore been suggested that in some way LSD mimics the serotonin and so blocks transmission between certain specific cells. Or it may be that the LSD in fact over-activates many cells. These effects may be restricted to specific areas of the brain. For instance it has been shown that LSD tends to accumulate in certain areas of monkey brain, especially the area responsible for vision.

One flaw in the serotonin hypothesis is that compounds chemically very similar to LSD, and therefore to serotonin, do not have the same psychedelic effects on the mind. Another difficult fact to explain is that LSD and mescaline have similar effects on the mind, and yet are chemically very different.

Mescaline resembles another brain transmitter, noradrenaline. However it is interesting that LSD users build up a tolerance to mescaline, and vice versa. This does seem to suggest that there is some common site of action.

Recently a group of scientists working at Yale University have found a group of brain neurons which are especially sensitive to LSD. The spontaneous electrical activity of these cells was inhibited by LSD. However whilst some of those cells were inhibited by mescaline, others were not. This emphasizes the incredible complexity of the brain's cellular chemistry.

The possibility of looking at the behaviour of individual brain cells has been recently opened up by the work of several research groups. For instance Sir John Eccles, working at Buffalo University, uses a microelectrode less than a thousandth of a millimetre in diameter to explore the electrical behaviour of individual neurons in living cat brains. At Boston Dr Hubel from Canada and Dr Wiesel from Sweden are using similar equipment to study individual neurons which are involved in vision. What is becoming clear from this work is that each neuron has its own specific task. It may even be true to say that no two neurons are identical and perform exactly the same task.

If the electrical activity of individual neurons varies so much, then it is also likely that their chemistry varies as well. One of the complex projects of modern biochemistry is to sort out the differences in chemistry between the brain's ten thousand million nerve cells.

Our increasing knowledge of the structure and chemistry of the brain has naturally led to fears that the information will be misused. So-called 'truth drugs' have received wide publicity. In fact most of these drugs, such as sodium amytal, are basically anaesthetics which cause drowsiness. There is no clear evidence that people under the influence of the drug are more truthful, any more than they would be while half-asleep.

Other writers have speculated that tranquillizers could be placed in a nation's water supply, so subduing an aggressive nation under the heel of a totalitarian regime. Mind-affecting drugs crop up repeatedly in the wars of science fiction. Indeed it is well known that amongst American weapons is the 'incapacitating agent' B2 whose formula is a closely kept secret. The toxic effects of B2 include mental slowness, disorientation, hallucinations and sometimes violent outbursts against other people. Another weapon already used in capturing animals alive is the dart containing a tranquillizer or sedative. Some have suggested that similar weapons could be used in warfare.

Some of these possibilities are certainly horrible to contemplate. However, one of the brain's best defences is its own complexity. It is very difficult to predict what effects a drug will have on a person, as we have seen in the case of LSD. As Professor David Samuel pointed out in a symposium on 'Science and Society' held in 1971: 'The complexity of the human mind is a sufficient safeguard against manipulation by a madman or a dictator.' It is only fair to add that other scientists at the same conference did not share Professor Samuel's optimism. As our knowledge of the brain's chemistry becomes increasingly detailed, it seems inevitable that new and more sophisticated drugs will be discovered to exert even more specific effects on man's behaviour.

This niggling undercurrent of apprehension is certainly not pacified by experiments at present being carried out using electrodes planted in both animal and human brains. The potential control of behaviour made possible by these techniques makes the very general influence of currently-known drugs on the brain look mild in comparison.

The implantation of electrodes in the brain was initiated by Dr Hess in 1928. It has now become a routine procedure. A small hole is made in the skull of the animal or man, and very fine metal electrodes may then be planted in specific areas of the brain. It is a curious property of brain tissue that it experiences no pain. More than 600 electrodes have been placed in certain areas of monkey's brain. Electrodes are attached to the skull, and have been left in both animals and humans for many years, with no apparent ill-effects. There seems no reason why they could not be left there for life.

By means of these electrodes simultaneous electrical recording can be carried out from many areas of the brain while the animals move around freely. In the earlier equipment their freedom was limited only by the length of the wires connecting the electrodes to the recording apparatus. Cerebral areas related to pain, pleasure, eating, sexual life and learning have all been investigated by these means.

The electrodes can be used not only to pick up electrical activity but also to stimulate specific regions of the brain. The effects of stimulation on behaviour can then be observed. Some parts of the brain rapidly become fatigued. For instance the motor cortex is a well-defined region in the roof of the brain which has detailed control of the muscles that produce movement. Within it are big neurons with long nerve fibres which carry information to the muscles via 'relay stations' deep inside the brain. The motor cortex of monkeys becomes tired out after only ten seconds of electrical stimulation. However other areas hardly seem to fatigue at all. The stimulation of one collection of neurons in the monkey resulted in various facial grimaces. This same stimulation was carried out no less than 250,000 times throughout a six-week period with exactly the same grimace each time.

During the past twenty years several techniques have been described for cerebral stimulation by remote control. For instance a radio receiver and transmitter, developed by Professor José Delgado, is about the size of a box of matches and weighs only twenty-two grammes. It is fitted on the skull and connected to electrodes embedded in the brain. One of these radio-electrodes, called a 'stimoceiver', has three channels for transmitting electrical activity, and three channels which can be used for stimulation.

This development means that animals can be allowed to roam freely, and yet at the same time be continuously monitored by remote control. At Alamogordo in New Mexico in 1969 a small artificial island was occupied by a chimpanzee. Experiments were conducted by Professor Delgado and a team from Yale University. On the chimpanzee's head was a stimoceiver with a two-way radio link to a nearby computer. Electrodes were connected to

B

the amygdala, an area deep inside the brain. Information about electrical activity in the amygdala could therefore be continuously beamed to the computer. Other electrodes were connected to the brain-stem where stimulation was clearly unpleasant to the animal.

The computer was then programmed to detect a particular pattern of electrical activity which meant that the chimpanzee was feeling aggressive. As soon as this pattern was detected the computer would send a radio beam out to stimulate the 'punishing' electrodes in the brain stem. After a number of periods of computer control the animal had been turned from a normally active chimpanzee to a quiet and docile animal. When the computer had been switched off it took about two weeks for the animal to return to normal.

Observers have been quick to point out that Alamogordo was the site of the first atomic bomb test twenty-four years before this experiment. No-one could deny that the advent of nuclear power has been misused. Many feel that the far-reaching applications of this kind of behavioural control may have no less sinister applications.

Already remote control techniques are being widely used in the study and control of animal behaviour. Dr Detlev Ploog, working at the Max-Planck Institute of Psychiatry in Munich, is engaged in a detailed study of the social behaviour of squirrel monkeys. The monkeys are organized into a 'dominance hierarchy' in which there is a dominant male and favourite female. However, by transmitting signals to certain parts of the brain, a normally passive male can be made to challenge the dominant male in a quite uncharacteristic fashion. The reactions of the other monkeys to this rather unexpected behaviour can then be assessed.

Various types of electrodes have been planted in the brains of humans. Dr Robert Heath of Tulane University has carried out experiments on a wide range of subjects living in New Orleans. These people have electrodes permanently fitted to their heads and are free to stimulate various parts of their brain by pressing different buttons. Not surprisingly one popular place for stimulation is a region deep in the front part of the brain where electrical stimulus produces sexual feelings. It should be emphasized that these subjects are free to carry on their daily work. There is no restriction to laboratory conditions.

Professor Delgado has already used stimoceivers placed in the brains of patients in a hospital where radio surveillance by a computer is possible. He envisages the possible use of a brain-computer radio link to control epileptic fits. As soon as information about abnormal neuron behaviour was received a signal could be flashed back from the computer to inhibit the fit.

Electrodes are being planted in human brains for very different purposes by Professor Giles Brindley of the Institute of Psychiatry in London. The aim in this case is to help blind people to see. A wide range of wires is planted in the back of the brain which receives signals from the eyes. By using various photo-electric cells, devices which convert light waves into electrical impulses, it may eventually be possible to give blind people the ability to recognize objects, and perhaps eventually to read.

Another recent innovation in electrode technology has been the development of the 'chemitrode'. This is like the normal electrode except that it allows the injection and collection of chemicals as well as electrical stimulation and recording, all of which may be carried out by radio control on free animals. This means that stimulants or tranquillizers can be delivered to very specific parts of the brain of an animal within seconds simply by the press of a button on a control panel within radio range. At the same time chemical samples may be taken from other brain areas whilst the animal is experiencing fear, pleasure, pain or drowsiness.

Clearly the possibilities opened up by these experiments are immense. The use of such techniques is still in its very early stages. In many ways the ethical issues raised by such experiments are similar to those which come from our potential ability to control our own heredity. How far should we go in obtaining information which may be used to affect radically other people's behaviour? There is no indication of any slowing down in the areas of brain research outlined above.

The present use of brain-computer links also highlights anxious questions which are being raised about brain research of a rather different kind. It has been known for some time that disembodied brains can be kept alive for days under laboratory conditions. Dr Robert White, a surgeon of Cleveland, Ohio, has developed a technique whereby the brain of a dog or monkey may be removed, cooled to 2°C for several hours and then joined to the circulatory system of a second dog. The brain has been shown to be still alive by its electrical activity and chemical turnover.

In other experiments entire heads were removed and also maintained by means of the circulation of other animals. At least to some extent the brains in these heads kept functioning as whole organs. At present the reconnection of a brain to the nerves of the body is technically impossible – Dr White speculates about the eventual transplant of a whole head to another body. As Dr Peter Stubbs remarked in the magazine *New Scientist:* 'The mechanism and nature of consciousness is hardly understood at all and the nightmarish situation that, even remotely, could arise within a disembodied brain leaves little latitude for such experiments.'

Such warnings seem particularly justified by the experiments of some Japanese scientists who recently succeeded in freezing a cat's brain for six months. The brain was then thawed out, after which it showed once again its characteristic electrical rhythms, even though the original cat was long since dead. This opens up the bizarre possibility of eventually being able to transplant a brain of an animal which died months or even years previously. However far-fetched the possibility might seem, it gives some idea of the kind of basic ethical questions being raised by current brain research.

No outline of brain research in the seventies would be complete without a brief survey of some current theories on memory. Many molecular biologists previously engaged in studies of genetics have now shifted their attention to a study of the basis of memory. This fascinating problem remains one of the big question-marks which hangs over the brain. How do we store information and then recall it years later? How do we remember?

Professor Wilder Penfield is one of many scientists who have used electrodes to stimulate various areas of the brains of patients lying conscious and alert though under local anaesthetic. As some areas of the cortex are stimulated sensations are felt from various parts of the body. In other areas patients hear the basic elements of sound – buzzing, ringing, and so on, but not music or speech. In other areas lights, colours and shadows are seen, but not people or things. However when the electrodes touch the temporal lobes at the side of the brain, then whole events and thoughts begin to flow through consciousness, more vivid and detailed than in normal recall. 'Doctor, I'm climbing up a mountain and my friends are at the top.' 'I'm at home washing up.' Flash-backs like this could not be obtained from other parts of the brain. Penfield therefore called this area of the brain the interpretive cortex.

Surprisingly the patient remains fully conscious of what is going on in the operation room during recall. Sometimes the same experience comes over and over again by the same stimulation. As the patient 'listens' and 'watches' he is moved again emotionally by the beauty and sentiments of the sights and sounds that he experiences. Yet the details of past experiences summoned by an electrode can no longer be recalled by voluntary effort hours later, or even sometimes after a few minutes.

Professor Penfield has suggested that we have the potential ability to recall any past experiences. However, the fact that some experiences may be recalled in this way is not proof that nothing is forgotten. What these experiments do show is that any theory of memory must provide for the storage of a directional, sequential series of events complete with sound, vision and colour! It is this kind of complexity which has led to the present situation where there are almost as many theories about memory as there are people investigating it.

In the classical experiments of Dr Karl Lashley, increasingly large portions were cut out of the brains of animals. Dr Lashley hoped that by doing this he would also cut out previously established memory. What he in fact found was that as long as some cells remained of any particular area, then the ability to remember still remained. It seemed that memory was 'diffused' throughout the brain, rather than concentrated in one particular spot.

The one exception to this general rule seems to be a region of the brain called the hippocampus. In 1953 several Americans underwent brain operations in which this part of the brain was damaged. One of them, called 'HM' in the medical literature, has not been able to remember anything, except for a few minutes, since the operation, though he can remember the main details of his life up to the time it happened. It appears that this area of the brain is necessary for implanting memory.

It seems fairly well established that two different mechanisms underlie the short-term memory and the long-term memory which we experience. I may hold a telephone number in my head long enough to dial it, though it will then be forgotten unless I continue to repeat it at regular intervals. The first type of memory storage seems temporary and the second permanent. In fact there seems to be a gradual 'handing over' of the short-term mechanism to the long-term, rather than a sudden change-over. For instance short-term memory may be erased by electric shock treatment, or by concussion – both treatments could have the effect of destroying reverberating electrical impulses travelling round neuronal networks. As time goes on the chances of memory being erased by these means becomes gradually less.

The permanence of the memory storage is one of the real puzzles that biochemists are currently trying to explain. How is it that an old lady of ninety may forget what happened five minutes ago, but at the same time remember vividly childhood experiences of eighty years ago?

In 1904 a scientist named Richard Seman made the radical assumptions that each stimulus that an animal receives somehow leaves a material trace in its central nervous system. He called this trace an 'engram' and suggested that it might be chemical in nature. Today the theory that long-term memory has a chemical basis is very popular. It is the nature of this chemical system which is so difficult to determine.

Many studies have been carried out on the acquisition of new behaviour patterns in animals, and the correlated changes which occur in brain chemistry. It has been shown that injected anti-biotics which inhibit protein synthesis will also block the formation of long-term memory. Acquisition of new behaviour patterns is still possible when brain protein synthesis is down to ten per cent of normal, but the memory trace is lost within a few hours.

At the University of Goteborg in Sweden Professor Holger Hyden and his colleagues are studying the chemical changes which occur in small groups of brain cells during the learning process. Their micro-techniques involve the analysis of chemicals obtained from only a few hundred cells weighing less than a millionth of a gramme. In 1970 they reported the discovery of a protein molecule, called S100, extracted from rat brains only after the learning of new behaviour had occurred.

The problem with these experiments is that there is no specific evidence that protein is directly involved in memory storage. Protein synthesis is a normal function of all living cells, and it is hardly surprising that there is increased synthesis during increased neuronal activity. Neither is it very likely that protein could be the specific storage chemical. Nearly all the protein of the brain is renewed every three weeks. A chemical with such a high turnover could hardly serve as a long-term store of information.

Another molecule widely canvassed in the sixties as having a role in memory storage is the nucleic acid RNA. This has a chemical constitution very similar to DNA, and is used in the conversion of the genetic information from DNA into the specific sequences of amino-acids which are necessary for the synthesis of protein. Some think that just as DNA contains the genetic information, so RNA could somehow code the memory information.

Dozens of research groups in the past ten years have attempted to show that learned conditional responses in an animal could be transferred to another animal by injections of appropriate RNA fractions from the nervous tissue. These experiments captured both the public imagination and the attention of the press. Planaria worms were chopped up and fed to other worms, which supposedly absorbed their learnt behaviour. Jokers started to suggest that a professor's chopped-up brain fed to his students might be a speedy way to learn.

In actual fact, despite several reports that transfer of learning is possible, the evidence is by no means conclusive enough to single out RNA as a repository of learning. Indeed there is much evidence that nervous activity and brain RNA synthesis are closely related. But since RNA synthesis is necessary for protein synthesis to occur, this may simply reflect the higher activity of the neurons during learning. Indeed it seems rather unlikely that RNA would act as a long-term information store because its rate of breakdown and re-synthesis in cells is normally very high.

An intriguing fact about nerve cells is that they do not divide. Cells which die are not replaced. Our brains physically start to decay from the age of about twenty-five on, though our intellectual capacity may go on increasing because of new learning. These facts have led some to suggest DNA itself as the storage molecule. Chemical alteration of the nucleotides has been postulated as a mechanism whereby the 'memory DNA' could be differentiated from the 'genetic DNA'.

Other theories suggest that the key to memory is the formation of new neuronal pathways by the growth of new synapses. Increased RNA and protein synthesis during long-term learning are therefore chemical reflections of this new cellular growth. Another suggestion is that the chemical nature of synapses might change during the learning process.

One of the most encouraging aspects of memory is that it is so stable, and the information stored in such a complex way. This means that literal brain-washing is not strictly possible using present techniques. Even though temporary brain confusion may result from lack of sleep, fear, constant bright lights, interrogation and so on, the storage of information in the brain remains the same. This is why some political prisoners who apparently give way to their interrogators during captivity will often afterwards change their minds when the pressure is off. Their basic beliefs still remain the same.

During the next ten years some big steps forward are likely in brain research. Discoveries about memory may eventually lead to specific manipulation of even this aspect of our personal experience. In 1971 it was announced that brain cells could be taken from mouse embryos and grown in the laboratory. They formed themselves into groups and continued to undergo at least some of the changes that occur in the development of the intact mouse brain just after it is born. Just as the genetic content of our cells may soon be manipulated in the laboratory, eventually perhaps specific information will be fed into our brains at birth.

Opportunities for speculation are endless. Already we can exert enormous power over the mind by the use of drugs, and potentially even more by the use of electrodes. By the turn of the century techniques of mind control may make even these advances look clumsy in comparison. Never before has man held such power in his hands. Never before has there been such a temptation to misuse it.

How brave the new world?

If the main characteristic of a god were his power, then it might seem that man was more like a god than ever before. It is man, with his religion science, and its high-priest technology, who walks in space watched by millions of viewers in what Marshall McLuhan has called our 'global village'. It is man, with his religion science, who fits people with new hearts, keeps people alive in machines, changes their minds or their sex. It is man who eventually, as we have seen, will have the ability to produce himself artificially and affect his own inheritance. It is man who can benefit from his own research with its potential for healing the minds and bodies of millions of sick people.

Nevertheless, despite all this, one of the most marked characteristics of our generation is a turning away from science as a panacea for all its ills. As John Maddox put it in a recent address to the British Association at Swansea: 'It is hard to imagine a more complete contrast than that between the way in which technical developments used to engender optimism and the way in which the prospect of technical innovation has now become a kind of threat.'

Even Dr Edmund Leach, whose 1967 Reith lectures entitled 'Runaway Man' certainly extolled man's godlike power over nature, wrote in 1971: 'If we continue to imagine, as we have done in the past, that humanity is the gainer every time that the technologists achieve a new triumphant feat of domination over the environment, then man's long-term future is bleak and lonely.'

Jacques Monod, Nobel prize-winner and author of the book *Chance and Necessity* discussed in chapter four, has spoken of the modern frustration which has 'led to the rejection of science as a pursuit and objectivity as a moral attitude'. In a recent international survey by Johann Galtung on 'images of the world in the year 2000', clear evidence was found of what he calls 'science pessimism' in the attitudes expressed by respondents from the most highly industrialized and developed nations. As we have already noted, there has been a turning away from science in secondary education. Political groups lobby scientists at international meetings. Whilst in many countries where science and technology are still just developing there is still an air of optimism, in those countries where it is already developed there is a general feeling of disillusionment. Why?

There are many reasons. One is simply that evil is still as rampant in our society as ever. No amount of science and technology, further education or raised standard of living has changed that. And, if we are to be brutally honest about the history of science during the past hundred years, there is no doubt that nearly every major scientific discovery has been misused. There is little evidence to suggest that, in this respect, the next hundred years are going to be any different.

As Hegel remarked long ago: 'What experience and history teach is this – that people and governments have never learnt anything from history or acted on principles deduced from it.' Or, as one well-known humanist, Margaret Laws Smith, has vividly put it: 'Collectively we are much more like two-year-olds in a petrol store with a box of matches than we are like gods or even responsible adults.'

The old addage that man's discoveries are neutral, and that it is only their application which involves moral choice, is at least partially true. When man discovered fire he could either warm himself with it or go out and burn the neighbouring villages. When he discovered iron he could either make cooking-pots or better spears for killing people. Drugs may be used to heal minds or break minds. Nuclear power may be used to warm your house or blow up a nation. The difference is one of degree, not of kind.

However, there is another sense in which science is never neutral. The picture of scientific research as completely rational and coldly objective is a myth. Science is a human activity and like all human activities it involves value judgments. Decisions have to be made about what projects are worth undertaking. Hypotheses must be evaluated. The tackling of certain problems may depend on the availability of equipment and personnel, and especially funds.

It might therefore be more accurate to talk of the potential of science for good or evil. No science is neutral, but some investigations are less neutral than others. Even the most sober-minded, level-headed scientist must feel some sense of uneasiness as he surveys the current literature and evaluates the potential for evil in the light of past history. Paradoxically it is often the scientist with the purest motives of healing sickness whose fundamental discoveries about the nature of life itself may potentially be so dangerous. 'It seems almost indecent,' wrote Sir Macfarlane Burnet who won the Nobel prize in 1960 for his work on tissue transplants, 'to hint that, as far as the advance of medicine is concerned, molecular biology may be an evil thing.'

But perhaps the most fundamental reason for the current disillusion with science is that it gives such a feeling of incompleteness. Many going through school and university feel themselves squeezed into an impersonal, technological mould which tends to make them less rather than more human. As one has rather quaintly put it: 'The scientific world-view makes you feel as if you've been conned. There's something missing.' The student ferment of the sixties was in part a reaction against the sense of alienation brought about by a technocratic society which wanted to put rows of people in little boxes and then stamp them with a degree at the end of the process. Many have felt man's very humanity to be at stake – his capacity for free-expression, creativity and self-determination.

One of the paradoxes of modern science is that while on the one hand it appears to give man god-like powers, on the other hand it appears to reduce man to another rather puzzling animal in a very puzzling universe. Books have been pouring off the press with titles such as *The Naked Ape*, *The Human Zoo* and *The Human Animal*. There appears to be no limit to man's ingenuity and creativeness in comparing himself with animals.

But is that all we are? Are we nothing but trousered apes who have hit it off rather well with our environment? Is the value of man based simply on the fact that he is more dominant than any other species? Are we just a passing phase thrown up by a blind whim of evolution? A bundle of conditioned reflexes pre-determined by our genes, chemistry and environment? One more digit in the computer of life?

Is science a god that has failed – and reduced its worshippers to nothing?

Chapter Two

MECHANISM AND MEANING

The story is told of a visit of the behaviourist psychologist Professor Burrhus Skinner to lecture at Keele University. After Skinner had given his formal lecture, in which he emphasized an objective, mechanistic description as a total explanation of man's behaviour, he was invited to have an informal chat with the professor who had chaired the meeting. Skinner was asked whether in fact he was at all interested in who he, the chairman, and others were. Implacable, Skinner replied: 'I am interested in the noises coming from your mouth.'

Commonsense dictates that this is absurd. And commonsense, in this case, is quite right. Why is it right?

One way of understanding the scientific method is to picture it as building models of observed data. For instance I may observe that all the cows in my prize herd start dying suddenly for no apparent reason. I may suggest several models, or hypotheses, to explain this phenomenon: for example that they are being shot by snipers in woods surrounding the field, or that dangerous cosmic rays are damaging their chromosomes, or that some virus disease is being passed rapidly from one cow to another. To test these various models I place my herd in a shed where they are shielded from bullets and cosmic rays. Since they carry on dying I conclude that the third model is the one that most nearly fits the facts.

Whether a model is a good one or not depends on the extent to which it is testable. Sir Karl Popper has pointed out that this is one way of determining what belongs to scientific discourse and what cannot in fact be tested by the scientific method. For example if I look at a painting and say, 'This is beautiful, it arouses in me a sense of awe and wonder,' no scientist, as a scientist, could possibly deny that I was right. Of course by his own subjective awareness he could disagree with my assessment of the painting. But no amount of placing electrodes in my brain, or monitoring my heart-rate, analysing hormones in my blood, or any other applications of the scientific method, could possibly prove me wrong.

On the other hand I could look at the same painting and explain the different colours on the canvas by suggesting that there were more copper compounds in the paints than iron compounds. This model can then be easily tested in the laboratory and proved true or false. The difference between the two models, or hypotheses, is that the second one generates questions which can be answered by objective measurement; the first does not. Only the second therefore is a valid topic of investigation by the scientific method.

Occasionally, to explain certain phenomena, models are put forward which receive great popular acclaim because they seem to fit together so many different facts. Unfortunately, however, on closer examination it may be seen that there are in fact *no* facts that could conceivably be found out which would not fit into the model. For instance I might put forward the theory that all my behaviour is explainable by the presence in my brain of conflicts between different 'centres'. One centre I call my go-go, which represents my basic aggression and sexual impulses. Another centre I call my super-go-go, which is roughly equivalent to my conscience. And underlying it all is the mysterious ado which is the basic source of my will to do things. My behaviour is governed by the degree in which the ado is influenced by the turbulent go-go or censored by the self-righteous super-go-go.

The beauty of such a model is that it could never be proved wrong. Whichever way I behave I could postulate enough different links between the various centres to 'explain it all'. At the same time, of course, and for the same reason, the model could never be proved right. Though having a certain aesthetic attraction it is doubtful therefore whether such models could be

called 'scientific'. There is also the illusion that by giving something a name we have therefore in some sense explained it and
so have more control over it. This perhaps stems from the ancient
belief that to possess someone's name meant to possess power over
them.

All this is not to say, however, that explanatory models may
all be neatly pigeon-holed as 'scientific' or 'non-scientific'. Science,
as we have already noted, is a human activity, and there is no such
animal as an uncommitted human being. Purely objective knowledge does not exist because there must always be an observer to
note the phenomena, suggest a hypotheses, and then gather and
interpret data. As Michael Polanyi has shown in his book *Personal
Knowledge*, the personal participation of the knower of that which
he knows is both pervasive and inescapable. There are no such
things as 'hard facts'. When the scientist suggests a model to
explain a certain set of observations he will limit his experiments
to those which could support or contradict the model. Constant
decisions of this kind means that the limits of his search will only
be as great as his models warrant. This means of course that the
facts found out will only be those coming within the limits of the
questions which the model itself poses. For instance if, to explain
the phenomenon of tides in the Atlantic, I pose the model that
they are due to the magnetic attractions of Europe and America
acting alternatively on the water, I am unlikely to be interested
in the movement of the moon.

The scientist is therefore involved in a series of value-judgments
in which he must assess evidence according to his past experience
and the current scientific literature. Furthermore it is well known
that great theories have often been adopted because of their
inherent attraction, beauty, depth or elegance. Einstein, for
instance, has spoken of 'the years of searching in the dark for a
truth that one feels but cannot express'.

Together with the personal involvement of the scientist is the
fact that his very methods of investigation will often alter what
he is observing. Clearly if I point a telescope at a star it is not
going to alter the star very much. But if I hit a guinea-pig over

the head with an iron bar its brain chemistry when I analyse it after death may well be different from what it would have been had it never seen the iron bar in the first place. These kinds of factors are most important when studying living systems. They are particularly relevant when trying to make psychological or physiological measurements on human beings. The trouble with people is that they know too much and are too suspicious by half.

Another complication comes when the scientist starts studying things which are either very far away or very small. Normally things we see are so close to us that the amount of time taken for light to travel from the object to our eyes is so small that it may be discarded. However when the object, such as a planet, is very far away, or moving very fast, then the speed of the observer relative to the speed of the planet has to be taken into account. It was this that gave rise to Einstein's theory of relativity. Again it emphasizes the important role of the observer.

When we want to observe something as small as an electron then a different kind of problem arises. To investigate atoms we can use streams of electrons. But there is no way of investigating electrons except by using methods which interfere with what we want to look at. This has given rise to Heisenberg's 'uncertainty principle' which states that we cannot know both the position and velocity of an electron at the same time. All we can do is construct mathematical equations which describe the probability that an electron will have a certain position or velocity at a given time. The role of the personal observer and the interference with what he is observing does not mean that science is therefore 'subjective'. It simply means that complete objectivity is out of the question. As Heisenberg himself put it: 'Quantum theory reminds us of the old wisdom that when searching for harmony in life we must never forget that in the drama of existence we are ourselves both players and spectators.'

We might therefore say that while all the true sciences are objective, some are more objective than others. The most objective are those which involve the fewest value-judgments and the least interference between observer and what is observed. A simple test of how 'scientific' a subject may be is to find out whether its main teachings are labelled according to the people who suggested them, or according to the observations which suggested the theories. For instance psycho-analysis is remarkably dominated by various schools of thought named after the people who invented them. However, very few of these theories or models of explanation suggest experiments that could demonstrate them to be either true or false. A characteristic of true science is that it is based on measurements which could be repeated by any scientist anywhere in the world provided that he is properly trained and possesses the right equipment.

Our view of science today is clearly very different from the rigidly mechanistic view of the nineteenth century. Then science was seen much more as the completely objective discovery of 'hard facts' which would eventually reveal the immutable 'laws of nature'. It was thought that science provided a literal description of an objective world. In fact the term 'laws of nature' was used in such a way that it almost seemed as if nature herself was compelled to follow these laws in blind obedience. The physical law of gravity was seen as the 'cause' of the planets moving in orbits.

As we have seen, this kind of naive realism is no longer tenable. We now realize that our scientific theories and models are useful representations of the objective world linking together various observations. But the model that we suggest is not the thing itself, nor does it make the thing do what it does do. As the philosopher Wittgenstein has put it: 'At the basis of the whole modern view of the world lies the illusion that the so-called laws of nature are the explanations of natural phenomena.' Our scientific models and pictures of the world may certainly become more refined in their ability to link up many different phenomena, but strictly speaking we could never talk of a scientific *proof*, as if there was something final and complete about the model that we were suggesting.

Now in pure mathematics we certainly could talk correctly

about 'proof' in an absolute sense because mathematics is a closed system. In other words it is we who define the starting-points and make up the rules of the game. In a game of chess I may check-mate my opponent's king, and no amount of juggling will un-check-mate him. The chess-board is a 'closed system' with its own rules that we have defined by prior agreement.

In science there is no such air of finality, or proof, because our techniques of investigation are open-ended. There is always the possibility that some new fact will force our model to be changed. As T. H. Huxley once put it: 'The tragedy of science is a beautiful hypothesis slain by an ugly fact.' And the fact that we observe something very many times does not mean that it therefore becomes more certain. For instance I may laboriously count a million white sheep, and on the basis of my observations propose the seemingly not unreasonable theory that all sheep are white. However the whole theory will be refuted by the observation of a single black sheep.

A remarkable example of this in the history of science was Newton's theory. This was indeed a beautiful model in that its ability to link together observations and powers of prediction were very great. For instance certain irregularities were observed in the orbit of the planet Uranus. According to Newton's theory these irregularities must have been due to the presence of another planet. Scientists worked out the exact position of where this planet should be. Sure enough, when the great telescope at Berlin was moved to the prescribed spot, there was the previously undetected planet which we now call Neptune. Such was the success of Newton's theory that it began to be viewed as a basic law of the universe.

But in the case of similar peculiar behaviour which was observed for the planet Mercury, no such gravitational disturbance could be suggested by Newton's theory to account for it. It was only when Einstein offered his competing theory to Newton's that the new model was able to absorb successfully the new piece of information. This is not to say that Newton's theory was completely wrong. Rather it was a question of refining the model to fit new observations. As with the white sheep, even though countless observations fitted with Newton's theory, a single observation which did not fit was enough to make a new model necessary.

Another characteristic of nineteenth-century thought was the strong feeling that the scientific method gave the 'real truth' about the world, and that any other kind of claim to truth was in some sense less than real. Indeed, this sort of thinking is still prevalent today.

Now the models that scientists put forward in attempts to conceptualize observed phenomena may also be pictured as maps. The point of a map is to make a representation of reality. It is not the reality itself, nor does it cause the reality. Whether it is a good map depends on how closely the representation corresponds with reality. Furthermore I may construct different maps to represent many different facets of the reality in a given geographical area. For example one map describes the territory geologically, another ethnically, another according to local flowers and animals, and so on. I need many maps to describe the area, simply because if I try to put all the information on one map it becomes much too confusing. The various maps are complementary. They describe different facets of the same reality. If the man who constructed the geological map said that his map was the only one that was really important, then clearly his view of reality would be a very lop-sided one.

The same principles apply in any application of the scientific method, for example in the scientific study of man himself. A biochemist studying man at a molecular level could, in principle, give a complete and exhaustive description of a human being in biochemical terms. Whether it would ever be a technical possibility is of course another matter. But even though the description could be exhaustive, it would still leave much to be said. To give a complete scientific picture we would still need the various investigations of the psychologist, the biophysicist, the physiologist and the anatomist, each giving their own particular descriptions using their own special language and methods. Considering that a complete mechanistic description of a man is therefore, in principle if not in practice, a possibility, would there in fact be anything left that we could say about man?

We should perhaps pause at this point and ask a simple question. When a computer works out a mathematical problem, do the electrical impulses flowing through the computer cause the problem to be worked out, or does the problem cause the electrical impulses to flow through the computer?

A few minutes' meditation on this question perhaps indicates that it is not as simple as all that. The reason is that strictly speaking the question is nonsense. It has no answer. The question is nonsense because it is trying to mix two kinds of language, the scientific description language of 'electrical impulses' and the purposeful language of 'working out a problem'. And when we try to mix two kinds of language together in this way then the whole idea of 'cause and effect' breaks down.

Now when I, as a conscious human being, begin to study another human being in a scientific way, I have begun to study him as an object. But in fact he is not just an object. He is also a conscious human being – at least I assume so because he behaves in the same kinds of ways that I do. I may therefore study the person's heart or his brain or his blood-pressure, or various things about the way he behaves. But I must do more than observe him if I am to understand him as a person; I must know him. This is because the way in which we use the word 'person' implies that we are referring to a conscious, choosing, human being. This is not to say that my scientific description is in any way incomplete in itself. It is simply saying that it gives only one aspect of the 'whole truth' that could be stated about the person. The 'whole truth' must also include the person's own subjective self-awareness of his environment with all that it entails in terms of rational thought, feelings, emotions and decision-making.

When I am making subjective statements about my own 'internal' world as a conscious being we can call this 'internal language'. When I make objective statements about other things we can call this 'external language'. The important thing is not to mix the 'internal language' with the 'external language' because nonsense quickly results.

We are back to our illustration of the painting. Does my experience of awe and wonder cause my brain chemistry to be in a certain state, or does my brain chemistry cause my experience of awe and wonder? The question is, again, nonsense. This is not to say, though, that there is no link between the two. While I was experiencing awe and wonder a scientist could be monitoring my brain chemistry, which may indeed change during the experience. My experience could be described both objectively in terms of brain chemistry and subjectively in terms of awe and wonder. The two accounts would be complementary and not in any way mutually exclusive. In no sense are they rival accounts.

The nineteenth-century feeling that science was giving the 'real truth' was therefore an illusion. Science, by the very definition of its own method, can never give more than one aspect of the truth about any given reality.

We are now in a better position to return to the question with which we began this chapter. Why was Skinner's statement absurd? The reason is simply that the statement took into account only the scientific description of words as physical wave-patterns in the air, and pretended that this was the most important account. It omitted the more important, though complementary fact of the subjective effect of the words on the conscious will of the hearer. The physical sound-waves of the words were relatively unimportant compared with their meaning.

We might, for instance, imagine a group of Martian scientists who came to earth and made a scientific study of chess. They could measure the size, number and colour of the squares of the chess-board. They could carefully analyse the movements made. They could note that the castles had turrets, the queen frills and the bishops mitres. But the meaning of it all, that it was a game, would elude any scientific description, just as the fact that a computer was working out a certain problem would elude any kind of scientific description of its parts, however complete.

Meaning and mechanism are two aspects of one and the same

reality. If I was standing on a cliff looking out to sea, expecting an important message, and I saw a light flashing morse code, the message could be readily interpreted. There could also be a parallel mechanistic description of the frequency and intensity of the flashing light, but it would not be very interesting. On the other hand if I was primarily concerned with making scientific measurements of all flashing lights out at sea the mechanistic descriptions might be very similar. However some lights might flash randomly, others in morse code. The first would have a mechanistic description only, the second would have the mechanistic description and the meaning as well, provided of course that I knew morse. If the message said that the cliff I was standing on was about to crumble into the sea, there is little doubt which of the descriptions I would deem the more important.

Determinism and free will

One of the most basic assumptions of normal people is that they are free. We may not think about it at all, we just assume it. If science suggests otherwise, then so much the worse for science. If my freedom is an illusion, then it is a very convincing illusion. Science should and does challenge popular assumptions of this sort. But the experience of freedom is a fundamental one!

This is not to say of course that we are free to do anything. If I jumped out of the window I could not fly even if I wanted to. I can only choose a chocolate biscuit if there is one there in the first place. My freedom may well be restricted by my physical situation, as it may be restricted in a different way by a repressive political system. But even though my freedom is not unlimited, this does not alter the basic fact that I am still free.

Now when we come to a scientific, mechanistic description of man there appears to be a problem. If, in principle, I could obtain an exhaustive scientific description of a man, including his exact brain-state and the positions of all the molecules in his body at any given time, would his so-called freedom not be illusory? Could I not say that his actions were completely determined?

Before tackling these questions in greater detail it is worth pointing out that no-one has actually succeeded in living as if they were completely determined, without becoming insane, or at least getting a headache. Indeed many have despaired at the thought that their feelings of freedom were illusory. For example one determinist, Steven Cahn, takes such a view in his recent book *Fate, Logic and Time*. As he rather woefully points out, if his theories or fatalism are true, then we are indeed confronted with a 'sorry picture of human life'. Yet so deep does our feeling of freedom go that we cannot avoid some concept of having responsibility for our actions. When I tread on someone's toe I might instinctively say 'sorry', even though I was inwardly blaming it on the irregularities of my brain chemistry.

Furthermore it is difficult to see how any consistent claim to complete determinism could logically be upheld. If I am completely determined, and therefore not truly responsible for my thoughts, theories or actions, my coming to a conclusion about something must also presumably be determined. But if I come to the conclusion that I am determined, then this conclusion must also have been determined. There is no particular reason therefore why I should value it as a conclusion more than any other conclusion. I have sawn off the branch on which I was sitting.

The same objection may be raised against those who maintain that our lives are predetermined by our early experiences between the age of nought and three. If it is true, then the putting-forward of the theory itself was presumably also determined by the person's early experiences between the age of nought and three. There is therefore no particular reason to suppose that it is any more valid than any other views that the person might hold, which were also of course originally determined by his early experiences.

These kinds of arguments have led many people to adopt a kind of schizophrenic existence in which intellectually they believe they are determined but in practice they behave according to their experience of feeling free. Apart from the strain of living with such a basic contradiction, there is also a subtle tendency to assume that while they are responsible for their good actions, their bad actions may be safely blamed on their genes, environment or the current state of their hormones. It is a case of trying both to have one's cake and eat it.

This position is not only dishonest, but logically false, for reasons that we will now try to explain.

As we pointed out in the previous section, things in science are not always what they seem. To take our everyday sense experiences and apply them to the very small or the very big (i.e. to 'extrapolate' them) is liable to lead to confusion. In the comforting everyday world of billiard-balls, I can shoot one ball at another and, provided I have enough data about velocity, angle and so on, predict which direction the two balls will take after impact. But if I try to extrapolate my everyday world to the world of electrons, then I find that they do not in fact behave like objects at all. In principle, there is no way of predicting what will happen when two electrons collide. This is not due to any technical incompetence in making a prediction, it is just that no prediction is in fact possible by the nature of what an electron is. The results of electron collision are physically indeterminate. In practice this does not matter very much because we can use mathematical equations to predict the probability that large numbers of electrons will behave in a certain way. But it does illustrate the danger of assuming that my everyday commonsense world-view is applicable in every situation.

In an analogous way, we might jump to the conclusion that because a super-scientist could in principle give a complete scientific description of the state of our brain, therefore our experience of free will must be illusory. Professor Donald MacKay, engaged in brain research at Keele University, has clearly shown this idea to be false. As Professor MacKay has pointed out, to demonstrate that my free will was illusory it would be necessary to show only one thing, that a prediction existed about a decision that I was about to make, which was binding on me whether I liked it or not. Clearly if such a prediction existed, then in no sense could I call myself free, because I would be limited strictly to that one predicted decision.

Now in fact no such prediction exists which is universally true and which I would be right to believe and wrong to disbelieve. Let us imagine that in five minutes' time I have to make the decision between marrying Susan or not marrying Susan. A super-scientist has a complete mechanistic description of my body, including my exact brain state, and is monitoring all the data going into my body and everything coming out. Of course we are nowhere near being able to do this in practice, but let us assume that it were possible. On the basis of his observations he predicts that in five minutes' time I decide to marry Susan. Let us now assume that he travels to the moon in a space-ship so that there can be no possible further contact between us before I make my decision.

Sure enough, five minutes later, I decide to marry Susan. When the scientist comes back from the moon he is suitably pleased that his prediction was correct. He also shows me a film of my brain-state before the time when I took the decision and explains the data on which his prediction was based. Though in retrospect I can agree that both his reasons and his prediction were correct, the peculiar thing about the prediction is that it has no universal validity.

Let us suppose that instead of flying to the moon our super-scientist had come into the room and told me his prediction. Immediately my brain-state would have changed. Furthermore the scientist's equations describing my brain-state would immediately be out-of-date because they would now have to take into account this new 'input'. Whether I believed the prediction or not it would still have the effect of invalidating it and making it out-of-date. Indeed after five minutes I could decide not to marry Susan after all. The scientist's prediction would not be such that anyone would be right to believe it and wrong to disbelieve it. It would not be binding on me. It would still have a take-it-or-leave-it quality about it. My future decision would be logically indeterminate. In a very real sense I would be free.

This might seem a very simple argument. In fact it goes very deep. It emphasizes the special role of the scientific investigator when observing another conscious agent as a conscious agent. It emphasizes the fact that however complete the mechanistic description may be of a human being, it can never give rise to a universally valid prediction about his behaviour. If the prediction were universally valid then anyone would be right to believe it. But in fact it has no validity for the most important person, the person who is himself making the decision, because if he believes it the prediction will automatically be invalidated. Putting it another way, I personally cannot predict a decision that I will make in the future; I can only make it. If I predict the decision, then I have already made it, so it is not really a prediction at all.

The crucial question as to whether a prediction could exist which is binding on my future behaviour is therefore 'no'. I am a truly free agent. I have a real responsibility for my actions. This is not because something has been 'left out' of the scientific description. It is part of the very real mystery of being a human being. My free will does not 'reside' in some particular part of my brain. It is an experiential reality which no amount of mechanistic brain-science could deny.

We should note that our arguments here do not depend on any particular theory of brain-science. We have suggested the farthest extreme possible, that the brain is as mechanistic as clock-work, to show that it does not affect the logic of the argument. However further research may well show that part of the brain's action is of a random nature, rather than mechanistically predictable. Clearly it cannot be too random in action otherwise we would be unable to experience enough rational thought to think about the problem.

We might sum up this section in the pithy words of MacKay: 'It is not people, but brains, that may or may not be machines. It is not brains, but people, that choose . . . and in so doing determine their eternal destiny.'

Life and soul
If many erroneously believe that scientific descriptions have somehow made our free will illusory, then there is no lack of

those who feel that the same descriptions have squeezed out any idea of man having a soul. However, the problems in this case arrive as much from misunderstanding of the word 'soul' as from a misapplication of scientific method.

The use of the word goes back to ancient times. In the Bible, for instance, it can be said that man *is* a soul rather than *has* a soul. No contrast is made between body and soul as if they were two 'different kinds of stuff'. The word is rather used in a very general sense to cover the various states of man's consciousness, including his life in general, his will and moral action, his source of emotions, and his physical appetite. It is also sometimes used to designate the individual or person himself. The soul is not therefore seen as an 'extra attachment' to our body, but rather as a word to explain the over-all pattern and purpose of our body's activities, particularly with regard to God.

The Greek view of the soul is in complete contrast to the Bible's view. Greek philosophers such as Plato have been summarized by the German theologian Professor Cullmann as saying that 'The body is only an outer garment which, as long as we live, prevents our soul from moving freely and from living in conformity to its proper eternal essence.' Death then 'looses the chains, since it leads the soul out of the prison of the body.' In other words the soul is rather like a captive bird held during the body's life, but which flies away to immortality once released by the body's death. As Cullmann himself remarks, 'The teaching of the great philosophers Socrates and Plato can in no way be brought into consonance with the New Testament.'

As Christianity moved from its Palestinian roots into the Greek world, it was greatly influenced by the Greek view of the soul. The systematic formulation of these Greek ideas came with Augustine (AD 354–436), Bishop of Hippo in North Africa. Augustine's view of the soul was very similar to Plato's, and his writings exerted a profound influence on the development of Christianity down to the present day.

As a consequence of these early influences the popular concept of the soul which has come down to us is a Greek one and not a

Biblical one. Naturally as science advanced to study man himself, and eventually man's brain, it was felt that somehow the soul was being 'squeezed out'. Soon there would be no room for the soul at all. Indeed, as early as Descartes in the seventeenth century, when traditional orthodoxy had to be reconciled somehow with the new science, it was suggested that there may be a 'pineal gland' which connects the soul to the body. Naturally others found that they had no need for the 'ghost in the machine' at all, and suggested that it was not just an illusion, but completely meaningless.

If the traditional Greek view of the soul causes problems for the scientifically-minded, the Biblical view does not. We have already seen how a scientific description may well be complementary with descriptions at other levels, particularly those which deal with meaning and purpose. The soul is therefore a 'meaning word' dealing with the over-all 'life' of a man, and not primarily with his mechanics. We read in Genesis that man 'became' a living soul, not that he was given one as an 'extra'. So when we are talking about the soul of a man we are talking about all that makes him different and significant as a human being, not about any 'extra bit' inside him.

What interests people today, however, more than the rather academic question of the soul, is the creation of life itself. In November 1970, Professor James Danielli announced the putting together of a living amoeba (a very small animal with only one cell) from the membrane of one amoeba, the cytoplasm of another and the nucleus of a third. This achievement was greeted by headlines of 'life synthesized in test-tube', and so on. No-one was more surprised than Danielli himself who, after all, had made his first transplantation of a nucleus from one amoeba to another as long ago as 1949.

The artificial synthesis of some kind of system which scientists could accept as a living system is still a very long time away. There is a big difference between taking cells apart, mixing together the bits, and then putting the bits together again to form new cells, and making a cell starting with simple chemicals. For a living system to be accepted as truly living it would have to have the ability to grow in some way, and then reproduce itself. It would not necessarily have to be a cell, but at the same time would have to have some way of stabilizing its internal environment.

Now most biochemists would accept that sooner or later it will be possible to synthesize some kind of living system artificially starting from basic chemicals. Whether it is scientifically worth it of course is another matter. The project has some enthusiastic supporters, notably Professor Charles Price, who in 1965 publicly suggested that the synthesis of life be made an American national goal. However, considering that in my body there are about 50,000,000,000,000 cells already, the achievement of the synthesis of one extra one, though undoubtedly a great scientific achievement, would hardly fill me with much enthusiasm.

What is more puzzling is the feeling still found today that if a scientist creates life then God has somehow been excluded from his rightful domain. Although, so the feeling goes, man has explained everything else, the creation of life is somehow sacred, and in some way a special act of God.

To show where the flaw lies in this type of thinking, we must pause for a moment and consider some different ways of thinking about God.

The pantheist believes that God is everything, earth, sky, sea, hills, trees, you, me and everything else. So he cannot talk about God doing something or not doing something. God could never be the subject of a sentence. He has no separate existence. Therefore we could never say that God has created the earth, because the earth is God.

Albert Einstein, who had a great sense of the mystery of life, was once asked whether he believed in God. He replied that he believed in Spinoza's God. For Spinoza God and nature were synonymous. Indeed Spinoza was expelled from the synagogue of seventeenth-century Amsterdam for his views. So Einstein was saying that he did not believe in a God who was personally distinct from him. God was everything.

This pantheistic view is often held by those who wish to

emphasize the sacredness of life. Indeed it has been used as an argument against pollution. However, the logic of the argument is somewhat dubious. For instance I might equally well argue that since a dog and a stone were both part of nature, and therefore of God, I would be perfectly reasonable in treating them both the same way. Furthermore, since nature had clearly put man in a dominant position, he would be perfectly justified in exerting his dominance freely, without holding back. What nature did, God did, and nature must therefore be right.

Another problem with pantheism is that it is difficult to find out what the word really means. The word 'pan' means all. 'Theism' is the belief in a personal, all-powerful, creator God. But when you put the two together they are in fact mutually exclusive. If you believe in a personal God then you cannot at the same time believe that he is the same thing as the whole of impersonal nature. Of course if you have been influenced by a culture with a theistic view of God, then the word pantheism would give an illusion of meaning. It would arouse in you certain feelings about nature. It would have the effect of making you project a sense of personality, inherent in the word theism, into impersonal nature. But really this is cheating, because there is no real basis in the idea that the pantheist is trying to put across for believing that there is anything personal or special about nature at all.

It is rather like playing the old national anthem in a country which once had a monarchy. Emotions are still aroused even though the last king has long since been dead. The word pantheism would mean nothing to someone who did not know what theism was. It would be like playing the national anthem to people in a country which had never experienced a monarchy.

Dr Francis Schaeffer has suggested that instead of the word pantheism, we should more accurately use the word pan–everythingism. But by this time we might indeed question whether we were saying anything at all. Perhaps it would be simpler, and more honest, to say that we had the feeling that there was something mysterious and rather wonderful about nature.

Another view of God which is very popular today is that of the deist. In fact a good proportion of the population of the West are probably practising deists without realizing it!

The deist view of God pictures him as a kind of gardener. The gardener takes a bit of desert and makes a garden out of it. He puts a wall round it to keep off animals, and he runs water channels from a reservoir to irrigate it. Then he puts in some complicated machinery to fertilize the soil, spray weed-killer and scare off birds. When all is finished he goes away and leaves it, but occasionally comes back to plant a few extra flowers or oil some of the machinery.

The more traditional picture of the deist view of creation sees God as a watch-maker who winds it all up and then leaves it to wind down gradually, with perhaps an occasional tinkering with the machinery.

This view was very popular in the eighteenth century. The idea of God was brought in to explain those parts of creation that could not yet be explained by scientists. Naturally as science began to explain more and more, the need to bring in God as an explanation became less and less. In our illustration of the garden, it was as if a man from outside had come in and gradually begun to understand all the machinery necessary for irrigation, fertilizing the soil and so on. Finally the whole system would be understood and there would be no need for a gardener at all. He might be dimly remembered as the one who started the whole thing off, but for all practical purposes he would be unnecessary and irrelevant.

The deistic feeling was neatly summed up by a celebrated, but probably legendary, conversation between Napoleon and the French astronomer Pierre Laplace. Napoleon remarked that Laplace had eliminated God from his astronomy. Laplace replied: 'Sire, I have no need of that hypothesis.' In other words, since astronomy had apparently explained all the movements of the planets, God was not needed to explain anything.

This feeling has come down to us strongly in the present day. Science appears to rule supreme. Many people think that there is some kind of supreme 'something' behind the universe, but if there is then he, or it, does not seem very interested in them. He may have started the whole thing off, but now he seems very remote, and somehow rather unnecessary.

So the artificial creation of life, according to this deistic view, would be one more indication that God was being squeezed out of his creation. One of his unique functions, the special creation of life, would be denied him. Man, with his religion science, would reign supreme.

We must look finally at the Christian theistic view. Here, as we have already noted, there is a belief in a personal, all-powerful creator God. According to this view, which is derived from the Bible, he has not only created everything in the past, but is actively creating everything now and will continue to do so in the future. Everything is held together and consists by his power. God is not viewed as an explanation for anything – rather there would be nothing for the scientist to explain if God had not first willed it to exist. He is not like the gardener who occasionally potters around in his garden. He is like the playwright who is actively creating all the structures and situations necessary for a continuing drama. Man's body, like the rest of creation, exists by the power of God. But of course, as we have seen, he has a real ability to choose. He is never a puppet.

So, in this view, even the atoms in the hands of the biochemists synthesizing life artificially in the laboratory would be held together by the continuing creative work of God. To suggest that God did not exist because man had created life would be as stupid as saying that Picasso did not exist because someone had made a copy of one of his paintings. To suggest that scientific descriptions of creation made God unnecessary would be rather like one of the actors in a play maintaining that the author of the play was not really necessary.

So with the pantheistic view the question of the creation of life just does not arise. There is no-one to create anything. With the deistic view there are certainly problems, because anything unexplained by science is looked on as a mystery, and therefore the domain of God. So one less mystery means a God that much smaller, rather like the fading smile of the Cheshire cat that Alice saw in Wonderland. With the Christian theistic view there is no problem because God is the active creator of all things. The mechanism of life is not as important as its meaning. When the Christian theist hears of the synthesis of life he may be moved to wonder at the intricacy of it all. But there will perhaps be no more wonder than at the sight of the last rays of the setting sun, or at a landscape of snow-capped peaks, or the sound of children's laughter.

Man the naked ape?

We have already remarked on the current popularity of books comparing man's behaviour with that of animals. In part this seems to stem from the idea that since man has made such a mess of both his society and his environment, perhaps a good look at his nearest cousins might furnish a few tips on successful living. The popularity of this kind of book may perhaps also be due to the very high regard with which animals are held by many in the West, especially those reared on Winnie the Pooh, Beatrix Potter stories or the more trendy Dougal. Or perhaps it is simply that most of these books on man's behaviour also contain a good dose of sex, which is not usually expected to lower sales.

But our main concern here is that the zoologist who looks at animal behaviour may be so carried away with animals that he forgets what man is really like. He becomes like the geneticist who gets so carried away with his science that he thinks that the control of genetic expression in bacteria must be the same as that in man just because the cells of both bacteria and men contain DNA. Such sudden extrapolations from animals to man are notoriously dangerous, and often are simply not justified by the actual facts.

The zoologists' comparison of animal behaviour with man's can easily become a typical example of a scientific model of explanation which begins to assume almost god-like qualities. And in the very act of becoming god-like the model ceases to be

C

scientific. This is a great pity, because at heart the model is a good one. Clearly there is a lot that is similar between man and animals. Their physiology, biochemistry and anatomy for example all have many points in common. Indeed, if they did not the whole of medical research would come to a halt because so much of it is based on animal experiments.

But when we start comparing behaviour we run into difficulties. Making behavioural comparisons is a very different kettle of fish from making biochemical comparisons. Dr Ashley Montagu, in the recent book *Man and Aggression*, has spoken of the 'fatal defect of extrapolation from animals to man'. The philosopher Professor Antony Flew, writing in *Humanist* magazine, speaks of 'two perverse yet widely popular theses'. The first is 'that men as they are now must in the last analysis be the same as their ancestors'. And the second perverse thesis is 'that all those differences of learned behaviour which so obviously distinguish one man and one society from another are relatively trivial and merely superficial, simply because all men are indeed much the same in their more animal functions'. Even more strongly the anthropologist Dr Edmund Leach has said that 'to argue that . . . the two behaviours are comparable in anything except a purely metaphorical sense is just nonsense.'

Why such comparisons can so readily become nonsense may be seen by noticing the differences between man and animals, and not just the similarities.

'I am a man' is one of the most profound things that I can say. It involves the power to conceptualize – to hold an idea long enough in my mind to think about it. It involves conscious self-awareness – the ability to look 'outside myself' and realize what I am. It involves the use of language which has been moulded and influenced by thousands of years of human activity. The fact of linguistic consciousness means that I can be both a subject and an object. I can think about my own brain mechanistically, and yet when it comes to my own choice know that it is not predetermined. As we have seen, nobody could make a prediction which would be binding on me. I am a free agent.

Furthermore my linguistic consciousness means that I can be genuinely creative. I can dream up ideas, create works of art and think thoughts which are genuinely new, which have never been created or thought of exactly that way before. I also have an incredible capacity for learning and memory, which is nowhere near matched by any animal. And I have the ability to adapt through the learning process and to communicate new ideas and learning experiences to my progeny, an ability also possessed by no animal. This means that I can read of man's learned experiences written thousands of years ago and they can still have extreme relevance to my own situation today.

All this is not intended to be a eulogy of man. It is just stating the plain facts about the situation. However clever a chimpanzee may be in learning tricks or getting food that is placed beyond its reach, it cannot retain an image long enough in its brain to think about it. An animal could never therefore imagine, calculate, predict or make a moral choice, because it could not conceptualize the ideas needed to carry out these activities.

These conclusions do not depend on guesses based on the way an animal behaves, but on careful scientific measurement. When we place electrodes on someone's head, we can monitor the various kinds of electrical waves that occur while the subject eats, sleeps, works out problems and so on. Certain wave patterns are characteristic of man's 'higher' functions such as conceptualized thought. Now when we carry out the same experiments on animals we find that, even when the brain currents are magnified as much as ten million times, only isolated and intermittent elements of these higher functions may be detected. The neurophysiologist Professor Grey Walter, who has specialized in these studies for many years, therefore concludes that 'the mechanisms of the brain reveal a deep physiological division between man and ape, deeper than the superficial physical differences of most distant origin. If the title of soul must be given to the higher functions in question, it must be admitted that the other animals have only a glimmer of the light that so shines before men.'

In other words, no ape could say 'I am an ape', not just because it cannot speak, but because it has no conscious self-awareness. All attempts to teach chimpanzees to speak have failed, not so much because of faulty vocal chords as because of the lack of the right kind of grey matter organized in the right way. It is not the size of the brain but its organization which is the crucial point. An elephant's brain is about four times heavier than a man's, but it does not possess conscious self-awareness. If it did we might not be here to talk about it.

We must not confuse language with communication. Most animals communicate in some way – even seals grunt under the sea, as you can find out if you listen in with the right kind of microphone. Bees have a very complex way of communicating to others where to find nectar. But it is human beings who talk. Indeed Sir Karl Popper has suggested that human consciousness is only possible with language, just as language is impossible without communication. The two go together.

In view of these fundamental differences between animal and man, the fallacy of making literalistic interpretations of human behaviour in terms of animal behaviour should now be obvious. Just two examples of the fallacy will suffice.

In the book *The Naked Ape* by Dr Desmond Morris, we read the following statement: 'The fundamental patterns of behaviour laid down in our early days as hunting apes still shine through all our affairs, no matter how lofty they may be.' Morris makes the claim that at the beginning of man's history there was an organization similar to that seen 'today in other species of apes and monkeys'. In this type of organization there was a single dominant male who kept order and gave the group security. The others in the group behaved towards the leader with due submission, the intensity of the submission being proportional to their position in the dominance hierarchy. Man's behaviour at this time was genetically determined for living in this 'natural tribal state'.

This theme is developed by the author in his book *The Human Zoo*. He suggests that the problem with man today is that he lives as a 'super-tribe'. He is forced to live in big cities where his old tribal pattern is broken down. This means that while his behaviour is programmed for the 'natural tribal state', he is in fact now living in a completely different situation. Life in the 'super-tribe' gives rise to all kinds of tensions, sexual abnormalities, aggressions, boredom and other problems. Morris suggests that man needs a bit more time (in the region of millions of years) to evolve into a new genetically civilized species. So he awaits the arrival of a whole set of genetic mutations which will enable us to be ourselves in the pressure of city life, simply because our behaviour would be the direct outcome of our genetical constitution.

Now there is little real scientific evidence for some of these speculative ideas. We shall be returning to some of them later in a different context. The main point here is the attempt to extrapolate from theories about animals to theories about man. And it is clear that the extrapolation in this case takes us far beyond the evidence that is in fact available. As we survey current anthropological data, one fact is abundantly clear – that there is no such thing as a 'natural tribal society', and neither is there any evidence that there ever has been. Every society has its problems. There is not a single case of a society whose 'genetic behaviour' is fully adapted to its environment. Whether it is a nomadic tribe, eskimos, aborigines, African villages or London and New York, every society has its tensions, its aggressions and its boredom. These have always been characteristics of human life, as can be seen from the earliest records that exist. Certainly the problems are intensified by the depersonalization found in big cities. But the so-called 'super-tribe' is not the cause of the problems – it simply tends to intensify problems which were inherent in man in the first place.

Another extrapolation from man to animals is the case of what Dr Morris calls the 'pair-bond'. 'In other groups of animals, whether they are fishes, birds or mammals, when there is a big burden for one parent to bear alone, we see the development of a powerful pair-bond, tying the male and female parents together throughout the breeding season. This, too, is what occurred in the case of the "hunting ape".' Now it is undoubtedly true that such bonds are formed amongst a wide variety of animals. As Professor Konrad Lorenz points out in his book *On Aggression* some of these, such as those occurring in the greylag goose, may continue for life, and are indeed most touching.

But it is equally true that there are many species which do not form pair-bonds. For instance the life of a chimpanzee is based on a shifting band society where groups of females seem to be the focus of group cohesion. In a normal forest population there is no evidence of permanent or even semi-permanent male-female relationships. The societies of hamadryas and gelada baboons are based on aggregates of harem groups, except when they are in certain special environments. And even within species, present-day primate social organization varies enormously. As Dr Rowell points out in the book *Primate Ethology:* 'There may be no such thing as a normal social structure for a given species.'

However, despite this, Dr Morris makes a direct extrapolation from animal to man and attempts to make a detailed comparison of the pair-bond with human marriage. Now we find among men, as we do among animals, a great variety of types of organization. There are some societies which practice polygamy, there are some which encourage the stability of the single pair, and there are others which lay little emphasis on traditional marriage at all. So what are we to say? Simply that there is a great complexity involved in human societies. It is absurd to pick out a few animal species which form pair-bonds, then speculate that this pair-bond formation was present in the extinct hominids which are supposed to have preceded man (a suggestion for which there is no scientific evidence), and then extend this pair-bond idea to the idea of marriage which happens to be best-known in our particular culture. As one reviewer put it: 'Adaptability through the learning process is man's great genius – why doesn't Morris just accept it?'

But further than this direct comparison, Dr Morris suggests from man's behaviour today that the trend towards marriage is 'only partially completed' and 'our earlier primate urges keep on re-appearing in minor forms'. In other words some of our behaviour is determined by the genes left over from our pre-decessors who supposedly did not form pair-bonds, and some of our behaviour is left over from our predecessors who did form pair-bonds. So when marriage does not succeed then it is the fault of our genes which come from the first group, and when it does succeed then it is because of the genes which come from the second group. Now apart from the fact that there is not a scrap of evidence for this wild hypothesis, it is a superb example of a model that could never be proved right or wrong. Whichever way we behave it could still be 'explained' by the model, since in our present state of knowledge we have no idea as to how much of our behaviour is in fact coded for in our DNA. In no sense therefore could we call this model 'scientific'.

Mechanism and Meaning

We have now seen enough to realize just how limited scientific models really are. As long as they are used according to certain simple rules, then their power to help us in interpreting and controlling our environment is very great indeed. But man's natural tendency is to become so dazzled with the new toys that these models give him to play with, that he begins to forget their limitations. As Professor Jacques Monod has put it: 'Modern society and technology live on science as a junkie lives on his drug.'

As man has become drugged with the success of so many scientific applications, the kind of mechanistic descriptions which science specializes in has dominated his thinking. With some people this domination has become so great that they have fallen into the trap of thinking that the scientific level of description is the most important one. Life has become 'nothing but com-plicated machinery'. Beauty has become 'nothing but physical sensations in my head'. Man has become 'nothing but an animal'. Mechanism has become more important than meaning. Just how mistaken the reasoning behind this thinking is we have seen in this chapter.

Yet more than this, scientific descriptions in general have not only been blown up out of proportion, but specific scientific models have been extrapolated to include all kinds of non-scientific data and ideas. As we shall now see, it is at this point of greatest exaltation that science becomes, most definitely, a god that fails.

Chapter Three

THE GOD THAT FAILED

You have been transported to Mars, and are being investigated by a team of inquisitive Martians. Being scientifically-minded they are filling in a series of long forms about you. Along with all the obvious things, such as date of birth and National Insurance number, there are some more searching questions. Do earth men think reasonably? You reply that they do, not necessarily in a coldly logical way, but that most people like to be reasonable about their beliefs as far as possible, and indeed that some measure of reason is essential for carrying out almost every activity of their daily lives.

At this point the questions start to become embarrassing. Could you make a list of all the things you believe, especially about mankind, your environment and the world in general? But, more than this, could you give precise reasons as to why you believe them? Suddenly, things become rather hazy. As you delve down to what you really believe, you find that you have no real reasons for believing very much of it at all. Yet when you finally get back to earth, despite your illuminating revelation, the chances are that you carry on believing exactly the same things as before.

Sir Karl Popper put this point in a nutshell in a recent broadcast interview, when he remarked that 'Everybody has some philosophy; you, and I, and everybody. Whether or not we know it, we all take a great number of things for granted. These uncritical assumptions are often of a philosophical character. Sometimes they are true; but more often these philosophies of ours are mistaken.'

Where do these assumptions come from? Clearly many of them do not come as a result of logically worked out arguments.

Most we absorb unconsciously from our cultural environment. Many are reinforced daily by the battering that we receive from the mass media. The reinforcement comes not so much from the content of the film, programme, newspaper, advertisement, magazine, book or whatever it may be, but from the presuppositions, or assumptions, which underly the content. Presuppositions are absorbed strongly simply because they are presuppositions. They are the sort of things that, if talked about, may be preceded with the words 'As everybody knows . . .' or 'All intelligent people know that . . .'

Now even though we absorb presuppositions so easily, we can still choose not to believe them. But usually life is so full that there is not very much time for thinking. In fact sometimes it seems that the hectic pace of modern life is all a sinister plot to keep us from using our heads. The end result is that everything is absorbed willy-nilly, whether there is any good reason for believing it or not.

Sometimes so many harsh facts begin to clash with some basic assumption that it is gradually dropped. A good example of this is the optimistic view of science held in the 1870s compared with the much more pessimistic view of the 1970s. One of the unspoken assumptions of the late nineteenth century was that science was inevitably going to make the world a better place to live in. It took the horrors of two world wars and the threat of a nuclear holocaust to blow away the remnants of that kind of idea. In other words the naive optimism underlying the assumptions could not withstand the test of time and the accumulation of hard facts which contradicted it.

One thing about scientific models of explanation is, as we have seen, that they tend to get blown up out of proportion. For instance the scientific mechanistic model of man has been put forward as if it left nothing else to say, though the fallacy of this position is clear, as we have seen. But part of the current reaction against science has been due to just this type of exaggeration. Just as the Luddites at the beginning of the last century went about smashing the machines that were taking away their jobs, so modern man has reacted against such mechanistic explanations because he feels that they are taking away his humanity. If the underlying assumption had only been realized as false, then the ensuing reaction might never have taken place.

In a rather different way scientific models of explanation have influenced a whole range of philosophies, political systems, ideas about language and religious ideas. Sometimes the scientific model has been superseded, but the system or idea to which it gave rise has carried on. Sometimes a single idea in a scientific model has been extrapolated until it has been made into a philosophical absolute which has been blindly accepted by millions of people as a basic assumption of their daily lives.

It is in such cases that science ceases to be merely a religion and becomes a full-blooded god. And, once again, it is at just this point where science becomes a god that it also fails most dramatically. Even though some of these scientific extrapolations have been absorbed as basic presuppositions by whole societies and nations, in the great majority of cases the acceptance of the validity of such an extrapolation is quite irrational – just how irrational we can see by looking at some specific examples of models that have been turned into gods.

Communism and causality

One of the characteristics of nineteenth-century science was, as we have seen, a very rigid view of cause and effect. Since the world was made of atoms, and atoms supposedly behaved like any other object, the whole world could finally be explained in terms of long chains of cause and effect at an atomic level. Similarly the movement of all the stars and planets in our solar system could be ultimately reduced to long causal chains. The atom itself, until the formulation of Heisenberg's Uncertainty Principle, was pictured with a nucleus like the sun, its electrons like planets circulating round it.

This ultra-mechanistic world-view has now given way to more modest claims. The principles of cause and effect still hold, providing that you are not studying things such as electrons. At this level you can only talk of probability, not of certainty. An electron still behaves like a particle from some points of view, but you need to picture it as a wave to explain other facets of its behaviour. The question now is not so much 'Where is a particle?' as 'What is a particle?'

Dr J. Bronowski, in a book called *The Common Sense of Science*, has shown how these very mechanistic ideas of the nineteenth century influenced the literature of the times, and gave it an air of fatalism. But it affected some political systems even more, Marxism being the most notable example. Marx tried to extrapolate mechanistic causality right out of science into a political theory. The essentials of Marxism now dominate more than one-third of the world's population.

This particular extrapolation has landed today's Marxist theorist with a major headache. The orthodox Marxist-Leninist has to remember that Lenin once declared: 'Marx's theory is the objective truth. Following the path of this theory, we will approach the objective truth more and more closely . . . From the philosophy of Marxism . . . it is impossible to expunge a single basic premise, a single essential part, without deviating from objective truth . . .' Yet today not only has the whole scientific world-view radically changed since 1867 when Marx published his *Kapital*, but there is abundant evidence that the kind of cause and effect that Marx envisaged simply does not happen in societies in the way he suggested.

Marx applied the principle of cause and effect by proposing that man was completely determined by his social and political environment. According to Marxist theory, just as man's body is controlled by the laws of nature, so in his thought and consciousness he obeys the laws of society. These social laws are in turn determined by the material processes of production and by the human relationships which arise out of these economic occupations of mankind. His existence and his behaviour are therefore directly determined by his environment. As Marx said: 'It is not the consciousness of men that determines their social existence but on the contrary, their social existence which determines their consciousness.' Marx's view of mankind was rather like the nineteenth-century view of the atom. Provided you knew enough about it you could predict accurately what it would do next.

So thorough is the Marxist concept of causality that ideas, or men or inventions, are seen as not only reflecting the social situation, but also as arising out of a causal necessity in society. In other words the need for something, or someone, is sufficient cause for a solution to be automatically produced. As Engels once wrote in one of his letters: 'That such and such a man and precisely that man arises at a particular time in a particular country is, of course, pure chance. But cut him out and there will be a demand for a substitute, and this substitute will be found, good or bad, but in the long run he will be found.'

In practice this aspiration to strict causality soon breaks down. A classical example is the story of Spartacus, one of Marx's favourite heroes in history. Spartacus was a slave who led a rebellion of gladiators a few decades before the Christian era. Beginning with seventy men, his rebellion ended with an army of seventy thousand which crushed the best Roman legions and marched on Rome itself.

Now the revolt of Spartacus, according to Marxists, had to fail, because the ideas of revolution that he was propagating were two thousand years ahead of his time. But if this is the case, then how did they arise in the first place? No revolt was called for at the time by the kind of historical or economic conditions which are supposed to precede a Marxist revolution.

The same problem arises when today the aristocratic and bourgeois intellectuals unite with the working class and help to lead it in its struggles. If it is 'social existence' which determines consciousness then in what sense could this action of the non-working classes be determined? One would expect a bourgeois always to remain a bourgeois because his bourgeois education and social relations have formed his consciousness. The Marxist answer is that the bourgeois can realize the laws that govern social developments and align himself with them. But in this case he is no longer determined by his social situation. He must be genuinely free to choose, despite his environment. Yet this itself contradicts Marxism. The principle of cause and effect simply does not work in this kind of way when it comes to people.

Neither is it true that a need in society automatically produces the answer to that need. For example Germany was ripe for revolution immediately after the First World War. Various socialist groups were calling for a revolution, and all that was needed was a man of Lenin's calibre to lead it and give the various groups unity. But the leader never came, and the revolution never happened.

Similarly, what are we to say of Stalin? According to Marxist theory Stalin's rule was inevitable. He met a specific need. His whole life was dedicated to socialism. He supposedly represented the vanguard of the proletarian class, the leader of a mighty socialist society. Yet Stalin also lied, killed millions of innocent people, and even murdered under false pretext some of the most prominent members of the socialist revolution in Russia. On 25 February 1956 the late Nikita Khrushchev denounced Stalin in a speech to the Twentieth Congress. He stated that 'the last years of Stalin's life became a serious obstacle in the path of Soviet social development.' Today the process of de-Stalinization continues.

In what sense, therefore, could Stalin be the inevitable result of a need in a society, and so good and essential according to Marxist theory? If it be said that Stalin was an accident of history, then how can we tell the difference today between 'bad' accidents and the 'good' predicted course of history? If we say that strict cause and effect apply in history, but that when it does not apply then it is an 'accident', what we are really saying is that strict cause and effect does not apply at all.

Clearly Marx's idea of causality does not hold water when applied in such a generalized way to society. Cause and effect simply do not produce the sort of historical progress that he envisaged. Understandably it does not form a part of the twentieth-century world view.

The illusion of a future

Ideas about human progress go very far back in human history. The philosopher Anaximander, writing in the sixth century BC, pictured the universe as originating in a chaotic fusion of hot, cold, wet and dry. These gradually resolved themselves into an orderly arrangement. He postulated that life arose in warm mud in the sea, and later gave rise to terrestrial organisms, including man.

Empedocles was another early philosopher, writing in the fifth century BC. He taught that the earliest living organisms were formed by the association of organs from plants and animals. Only those adapted to their environment survived. There was therefore a progressive replacement of imperfect forms by perfect forms as a result of the selection of these random combinations.

Other ideas suggesting development and progress have been put forward at various times in human history. These ideas crystallized in the nineteenth century with the biological theory of evolution. In the first half of the century Sir Charles Lyell produced *The Principles of Geology* in which he suggested that the earth's development had been a gradual process, and that fossils were the remains of animals millions of years old. An anonymous book came out in 1844 called *The Vestiges of the Natural History of Creation*. The author was later found to be Robert Chambers, the man who gave his name to *Chambers' Encyclopedia*. Chambers, though not a scientist himself, extended the idea of evolution from geology to the whole of animal life.

When Charles Darwin published *The Origin of Species* in 1859 it was therefore an attempt to give a more scientific basis to ideas about evolution which were already freely circulating. Darwin's own grandfather had in fact held a theory of evolution. The distinctive feature of *The Origin of Species* was that Darwin postulated a 'natural selection' in which those animals or plants which were best adapted to their environment were the ones which survived, though it is intriguing to compare these apparently new ideas with those of Empedocles writing more than two thousand years before.

The debate about biological evolution continues to the present day. What is more striking is the bizarre range of political theories and ethical systems which evolution has been invoked to support. As the idea of evolution was popularized, so the distinction between biological evolution and an evolutionary philosophy became less clear. Not content with a scientific theory, many tried to inject the ideas of struggle and progress, which were apparently inherent in the idea of evolution, into other realms of life. For instance capitalists justified big business by saying that if the weak suffered, then it was only a reflection of a natural process.

Karl Marx read *The Origin of Species* in 1860 and commented that 'Darwin's book is very important and serves me as a basis in natural science for the struggle in history.' Later on he asked if he could dedicate his *Kapital* to Darwin, but permission was refused. However, evolutionary ideas of causality and progress certainly left their mark on communist doctrine.

The fact that biological evolution has been extrapolated to support two mutually exclusive systems – communism and capitalism – perhaps says more for the ingenuity of politicians than for any political ideas which are inherent in the theory of evolution itself.

Another impression given by the biological theory of evolution was that it appeared to provide a scientific basis for the philosophy of progress, already widely held at that time. This air of optimism dominated the latter part of the nineteenth century and the first part of this century. Somehow it seemed as if man was going somewhere. He was not only evolving biologically, but there seemed great scope for realizing his full potential and for building a better society through a moral and ethical evolution.

Some of these optimistic ideas have filtered down to us today, though they are hardly popular, for reasons that we have already outlined. For instance H. J. Muller has suggested in *The Humanist Frame* that 'man will find one horizon after another coming into view on his triumphant marches of conquest over the interminable reaches of external nature and the similarly inexhaustible immensities lying concealed within his very own being'.

Sir Julian Huxley attempts to make a direct extension from biological evolution to ideas about human progress. In his view human cultural and biological evolution are 'two phases of the same process separated by a critical point'. Professor C. H. Waddington shares the same view when he writes that 'the capacities with which man's evolution has endowed him are an immensely extended carrying forward of the main progressive lines of pre-human evolution into radically new realms.'

For Julian Huxley these 'radically new realms' include giving evolution an almost mystical status as the central dogma of a new religion. The long-term concern of this religion 'must be to promote further evolutionary improvement and to realize new possibilities'.

At this point Huxley comes very close to the ideas of the French Jesuit priest and palaeontologist Teilhard de Chardin. Indeed Huxley wrote the Foreword to the English translation of Teilhard de Chardin's main work *The Phenomenon of Man*. Teilhard postulates a human ascension in evolution which eventually leads to an 'Omega point' of the universe. The 'Omega point' is described by Teilhard as 'a superior form of pantheism' when God will be 'all in all'.

One of the more far-fetched extrapolations from biological evolution has been the suggestion that it gives rise to an ethical system. This idea has often been integral to views of human progress. Huxley, for instance, maintains that evolution is good. Therefore it should be allowed to continue, and if possible be controlled by man himself. In a lecture published under the title *Evolutionary Ethics* Huxley suggests that traditional values of morality can be justified according to a respect for human individuality, the necessity for co-operation between man and man, and the new possibilities that cultural evolution may bring forth.

Similar ideas have been put forward by the biologist Dr Simpson, who states: 'As a first proposition of evolutionary ethics derived from specifically human evolution it is submitted that promotion of knowledge is essentially good.' In other words because cultural evolution involves increased knowledge, so increased knowledge must be essentially good for mankind.

All of these ideas of progress and ethics have a curiously dated feel about them. One cannot avoid the impression that they represent a last-ditch attempt to inject a little nineteenth-century optimism into the uniformly grey world of twentieth-century pessimism.

First of course no Utopian ideas have ever come to fruition in reality. As Leslie Paul has pointed out: 'Not one single Utopian exercise, not Thomas More's *Utopia* or Francis Bacon's *New Atlantis* or William Morris's *News from Nowhere* or Edward Bellamy's *Looking Backward* or H. G. Wells *A Modern Utopia* or G. B. Shaw's *Back to Methuselah* succeeds in predicting a future state of affairs remotely resembling anything which has actually come about or seems likely to now.' All such Utopian ideas seem condemned by history to a future which never arrives.

Some have held on to optimistic ideas for a life-time until their illusions were finally shattered by the sheer weight of facts about the human situation which suggested otherwise. H. G. Wells was an optimist and Utopian for most of his life, yet finally in *The Mind at the End of its Tether* broke out in protest against a seemingly unpleasant and senseless universe. For Wells it took a world war and the rise of Fascism before the spell of Utopianism was broken.

The futility of trying to extract an ethic from a particular scientific model – the biological theory of evolution – has also been pointed out by many critics. In a recent book entitled *Evolutionary Ethics* Professor Anthony Flew attacks the irrational thinking which tries to extract ethics from scientific theories. As Flew points out, it is simply not possible to say that something 'ought' to be the case simply because something else 'is' the case. No amount of knowledge by itself could dictate what ought to happen in any given situation.

The loose thinking behind this 'naturalistic fallacy', as it has been called, may be seen when we start asking specific ethical questions of biological evolution. Which aspect of evolution should we emphasize? The seeming carnage of life which the theory demands to produce a single dominant species? Or should we underline the balance and co-operation in nature which leads to the dying out of creatures with inefficient genes? Is Vietnam evolutionarily preferable? Perhaps the flood of refugees from East Pakistan into India was a good thing because the subsequent malnutrition, war and death led to an improvement of the genetic stock? Perhaps medical aid should be withheld from underdeveloped countries to allow those with healthy genes to become dominant?

The horror of such questions underlines the intrinsic absurdity of the arguments involved. As Ronald Hepburn wrote in *Objections to Humanism:* 'The evolutionary processes through which life and mind have developed are themselves entirely mindless and purposeless, and nature's "hospitality" is of a drastically limited kind.' Ethics are no more involved in the processes of evolution than in the sound of the wind in the trees.

The ultimate test of ideas about human progress is the simple question: 'Is any progress in fact taking place?' But as soon as we ask this question we have to ask the further question, 'What do we mean by progress, and how do we measure it?' If it is claimed that increased knowledge in itself is a sign of human progress, by what standard can one arrive at this conclusion? Certainly it is not an idea which can be logically derived from evolutionary theory. In fact no idea of progress may possibly be introduced without first making a value-judgment. According to evolutionary theory, what happens is what is, and there is no more to be said than that. There is mechanism but no meaning. Any idea of progress must be imposed by a human assessment which involves a moral judgment.

Interestingly enough, Huxley himself parts company with many biologists in suggesting that human biological evolution is at an end. Evolutionary theory suggests that the more adapted an organism is to its environment the less likely will be the possibility of change. Huxley maintains that since man has such great flexibility in his adaptation there is little likelihood of change. The argument depends upon logical possibilities rather than biological evidence. Certainly there is no evidence of any marked biological change occurring in man's make-up during his short history; nor according to evolutionary theory would one expect there to be. Indeed it is arguable that the genetic stock is in fact being lowered by increased medical care so that defective genes are now being passed on by those who would previously have died at an early age. Furthermore one effect of war is to eliminate the healthy and preserve those deemed medically unfit for active combat. Yet if, outside deliberate genetic engineering, the chances for human biological change are small, Huxley believes that the potential for cultural, or as he calls it 'psychosocial' evolution, is enormous.

Undoubtedly the past few centuries have seen a vast increase in knowledge. For instance in the last three hundred years the number of active scientists and the production of published papers have doubled every ten or twenty years. Many scientists spend up to half their time trying to keep abreast of new findings, let alone trying to find out new things themselves. There are already around six million scientific communications, and these are increasing at the rate of half-a-million a year.

Dr Robert Hilliard has pointed out that at the rate at which knowledge is growing, using the word knowledge in its broadest sense, by the time the baby born today graduates from university, the amount of knowledge in the world will be four times as great. By the time that same child is fifty years old, the amount of knowledge will be thirty-two times as great, and 97 per cent of everything known in the world will have been learned since the time he was born.

But in spite of this 'knowledge explosion', has mankind in fact made any real advance, according to any of the normal human assessments of progress? Are his moral qualities any greater? Is there increased happiness? Is there a greater cohesion in society? Does man now more easily get on with his neighbour? Is there less selfishness? Is there less suffering?

By any or all of these criteria, it is certainly difficult to establish any convincing progress which parallels the startling increase in man's knowledge. Clearly the standard of living of a segment of the world's population has increased dramatically. About 40 per cent of the world's resources are used by only 6 per cent of the population – those residing in the USA. While a good proportion of that 6 per cent eat too much, about one-third of the world's population suffers some form of malnutrition. Despite all the publicity, the pricking of consciences and the rattling of collecting tins, the harsh fact remains that the gap between the haves and the have-nots is growing ever wider.

Dr John Bryant has pointed out in his comprehensive survey entitled *Health and the Developing World* that the medical situation, both absolutely and proportionally, is in many countries worse than it was twenty years ago. He concludes that for half the world's people there is in fact no health service at all. While the medicine of affluent western countries becomes increasingly complex and expensive, so the most basic preventive medicine is still lacking from vast tracts of the world's rural areas. Whereas the annual expenditure for health per person in the USA is £80, and in the UK £22, in Thailand it is 24p, in Nigeria 20p, in Indonesia 8p, and in Laos about 3p.

If human sharing does not seem to have made much progress, then neither does the lessening of human aggression. Robin Clarke has estimated in his book *The Science of War and Peace* that some 400 million people will be killed in wars in the present half-century if present trends continue. He shows how the number of people killed through warfare has increased by a steady progression through the past few centuries. Some would question his figures, but none could disagree with the general trend. To suggest that man is becoming more peaceful is simply an illusion. As Bertrand Russell observes in volume 3 of his autobiography, when admitting disillusion about the basis for much of his anti-war effort: 'I had discovered an important political fact that is often overlooked, as it had been by me: people do not care so much for their own survival – or indeed that of the human race – as for the extermination of their enemies.'

Somehow the words of the nineteenth-century philosopher John Stuart Mill jar when placed in the context of the late twentieth century. 'All the grand sources . . . of human suffering are in great degree, many of them almost entirely, conquerable by human care and effort.' What Mill failed to realize was that it is not the quantity of human resources which makes the difference, but the will to apply those resources to human need.

What then of the countries which have the highest standards of living, level of education, medical care and opportunities for leisure? Should we not expect, with such an improvement of the environment, that man would blossom into fulfilment with a much more advanced development of his capabilities? A glance at those countries with the highest standards of living hardly sustains the thesis.

Happiness is very difficult to measure. But there are certain things which serve to show the extent of malaise in a society. Certainly the USA is one nation which has more of most things than any other nation. Yet in 1970 there were 15,000 people murdered, an average of 40 killings a day. More than one-quarter stemmed from feuds between relatives or friends, while in Britain as many as half the murders are 'family affairs'. The odds that you will be murdered, robbed, raped or beaten in the US had grown in 1971 to 1 in 36, two and a half times greater than 10 years previously. The total crime volume had spiralled by 176 per cent in 10 years, though the population had increased by only 13 per cent. In Britain, too, spiralling crime-rate figures in the second half of the twentieth century reflect the fact that a crime is committed on average once every twenty seconds.

If improved education and standard of living seem to make little difference to the crime-rate, neither do they seem to bring a new quality or purpose to people's lives. Together with the physical pollution which characterizes a modern technological society, there seems to be a mental pollution which takes its toll in breakdown, suicide, family instability and dependence on alcohol and drugs. In Sweden, which has the highest standard of living in the world, suicides have increased from 23 per 100,000 of the male population in 1950 to 40 per 100,000 in 1968. In Britain the National Association for Mental Health estimates that one in six girls now at school and one in nine boys may expect to spend part of their lives in a mental hospital. More working days are lost through mental problems than for influenza, the common cold and the whole range of accidents. Though in Britain the over-all suicide rate has gone down, Professor Mills, Professor of Investigative Medicine at the University of Cambridge, has pointed out that suicide attempts have increased by two-and-a-half times in the ten years from 1961 to 1971. It seems that many more people are now using attempted suicide as a silent plea for help in their despair, rather than as a serious attempt to kill themselves.

To cite more statistics would be tedious. What is perfectly clear is that however wonderful man's so-called cultural evolution may have been, it does not seem to have touched any of his deeper problems, and no possible progression can be outlined which is leading inexorably upward to some kind of higher state. The facts of the situation simply do not allow it. Some optimistic evolutionists talk as if man's psychosocial evolution only began in the nineteenth century when it was first thought of. But of course if the kind of development that they maintain occurs, then it must have been occurring since man's history began. It is just this long-term historical development which is so singularly lacking. Kingdoms come and go. Empires rise and fall. Ideologies wax and wane, but man plods on much the same, and his hopes, joys, fears, sadness, aggression, love, selfishness and despair characterize the laws, lives and literature of men of all civilizations since written records have existed.

Many ancient writings have a curiously modern ring. In the Sumerian *Epic of Gilgamesh*, of which the earliest known text is dated around 2000 BC, Enkidu cries:

'In my city man dies, the heart is oppressed,
Man perishes and the spirit is heavy.'

In an early Egyptian lyric poem there is the debate of a would-be suicide with his *ka* (a double of oneself). The *ka* suggests a surrender to the life of pleasure, but the one attempting suicide finally bursts out in indignation:

> 'To whom do I speak today?
>> One's fellows are evil,
>> There is no love in the friends of today.'

The prophet Hosea, speaking out against the corrupt society of eighth century BC Hebrew civilization, protested, as many do today, that every level of society was affected, and even nature itself was being ravished by such moral pollution:

> 'There is swearing, lying, killing, stealing, and committing adultery,
> they break all bounds and murder follows murder.
> Therefore the land mourns,
> and all who dwell in it languish,
> and also the beasts of the field,
> and the birds of the air,
> and even the fish of the sea are taken away.'

The world's earliest legal systems show that crime has always been part and parcel of human existence. Hammurabi, king of Babylon, set up a column inscribed with 282 articles of his legal code in the last year of his reign in 1751 BC. The code was especially concerned with human and sexual relations, and included all the main offences with which modern law is concerned, such as theft, assault, usury, debts and so on.

As our knowledge of early civilizations has reinforced the belief that 'there is nothing new under the sun', so modern anthropology has undermined the myth that there is anything intrinsically different between the nature of so-called 'primitive tribal' man and 'advanced technocratic' man. As the anthropologist Dr Stephen Fuchs points out: 'Primitive man lacks nothing of the mental faculties and abilities which modern civilized man possesses. Though some of these faculties may still lie dormant and be undeveloped, they are not lacking.'

All the evidence suggests that man, in whatever age or environment, is basically the same. The illusion of a future is just this – to suppose that man's nature in the future will be fundamentally any different from what it has been in the past. Certainly no such conclusion can be drawn from the biological theory of evolution.

The origin of religion

Another powerful feeling engendered by the theory of evolution is the general belief that if certain phenomena can be linked together in some kind of progression, then something has been gained in terms of scientific accuracy. This feeling even led certain German theologians in the last century to rearrange the order of the documents of the Old Testament according to an evolutionary sequence, even though there was not in fact a scrap of real evidence to support the rearrangement!

Similarly the same feeling has been used to suggest that the origin of religion could be explained according to an evolutionary process. What is so surprising is not so much that the theory was originally put forward, but that it still crops up so regularly in literature which claims to be scientific, despite the fact that there are no facts which actually support it as a model of explanation. The tenacity with which such theories may be held in popular thinking is an indication of the power that scientific models can wield in moulding ideas quite outside the scope of their original frame of reference.

These ideas about the origin of religion may be traced back to President de Brosses, a contemporary of Voltaire in the eighteenth century, who put forward the idea that religion originated in fetishism. The ideas about fetishism current at the time came from the observations of Portuguese sailors, who claimed that fetishes were animals and inanimate objects worshipped by the coastal Negroes of West Africa. Indeed the word fetish comes from the Portuguese word *feitico* meaning a manufactured object. It is now known that the fetishist has in fact a highly developed idea of God, gods, ancestors and spirits, together with a central belief in an impersonal power which is conceived to be effective every-

where in the universe. It is this all-pervading power which is seen
to be concentrated in the fetish, which may be a certain object,
person or place. The fetish is not an idol or a god to be
worshipped, but a link between an individual and the spirit-world
which can be used to liberate power for either good or evil
purposes. Fetishes therefore play a role in a complex system of
magic rather than in any rites of religion.

This much fuller understanding of fetishism which twentieth-
century anthropology has given us was unknown in the days of
President de Brosses. His ideas were taken up and developed by
the philosopher Comte, who died in 1857, just two years before
Darwin published his *Origin of Species*. Comte suggested that
fetishism developed into polytheism, and then finally into monotheism. With the popularity of evolutionary ideas in the late
nineteenth century this model gained rapid acceptance. The
well-defined development from one stage to another held much
attraction for those becoming used to neat evolutionary trees and
the idea that one species could evolve into another.

There were a number of variations on the same theme. Edward
Tylor, who in 1898 became the first Professor of Anthropology
at Oxford, saw the roots of polytheism in animism. He suggested
that from the animistic idea of all objects having a spirit behind
them sprang the idea of many gods responsible for various
natural phenomena, such as rain, thunder, wind, earth, fire and
so on. The highest level of religion was reached in monotheism.

Others, such as Robertson Smith, Frazer and Freud, saw the
starting point for this evolutionary process in totemism. The word
'totem' is derived from various tribal words meaning 'a close
relation' or 'relation by kinship'. Contrary to popular belief, the
totem is not the object of worship by the members of its clan, but
rather is felt to be a kind of guardian spirit which helps in maintaining group cohesion. It may be an animal or plant or even an
inanimate object. In some tribes totemistic ideas are linked with
various industrial or economic activities, while in others every
part of life is influenced by totemism. As with fetishism the
totem represents a link with a dynamic world view, and

again is therefore less connected with religion than with magic.

Ideas about magic in general were seen as the source of religion by other nineteenth-century writers. According to Sir George Frazer primitive man believed that all that happens takes place by personal or impersonal powers. These powers could be met by magic. When magic was ineffective, man then sought to approach the personal powers with prayer and sacrifice, and this was the source of religion.

Underlying all these various theories the same idea is present – that some kind of development had led inexorably upward from so-called 'primitive' ideas to a final 'higher' belief in one true God. A classic book which put forward this central thesis was the influential *Introduction to the History of Religion* written by F. B. Jevens and published in 1896. At the time Jevens was a lecturer in philosophy at the University of Durham. Similar ideas were popularized by Frazer's *The Golden Bough*. From such books evolutionary ideas about religion have filtered into quite recent literature.

Some have rather unkindly remarked that if the analogy with biological evolution was being taken seriously, then one would expect a development from the simple to the complex. Evolutionary ideas about religion are suggesting just the reverse, a development from the complex to the simple.

In actual fact the extrapolation from biological evolution to evolutionary ideas about the origin of religion simply does not hold water in the light of modern anthropological research. This has been clearly demonstrated by Professor Evans-Pritchard, Professor of Anthropology at the University of Oxford, in his book *Theories of Primitive Religion*. Commenting on Jevens *Introduction to the History of Religion*, he writes: 'I only instance the book as the best example I know for illustrating how erroneous theories about primitive religions can be, for I believe it would be true to say that there is no general, or theoretical, statement about them in it which would pass muster today.'

One of the characteristics of early theories about the origin of religion was that they were put forward by arm-chair speculators who had little knowledge of the peoples they were talking about. As Evans-Pritchard points out: 'It is a remarkable fact that none of the anthropologists whose theories about primitive religion have been most influential had ever been near a primitive people.' It was not until the 1920s and 1930s that detailed field work carried out on many hundreds of tribal peoples made earlier ideas untenable.

First, it was clearly shown that the concept of a supreme God, higher and more powerful than local deities or magical powers, was deeply embedded in the religious ideas of many tribes. Andrew Lang pointed out that 'the conception of a creative, moral, fatherly, omnipotent, and omniscient God is found among the most primitive people of the globe.' In many cases this God was thought of in personal terms rather than as a spirit. Such ideas extend from Aljura of the Aranda in Australia, to Mbori of the Azanda or Unkulunkulu of the Amazulus in Africa, while the idea of a Supreme Being is especially strong among the Arctic hunting tribes.

Some tribes, such as the Yuin and other south-east Australians, together with the Hottentots of South Africa and the Blackfoot Americans of North America, believe that their ancestor was the first man. His symbol is the moon or some other object connected with the moon. Sometimes he is confused with the Supreme Being and worshipped in his place. Crude images of this First Father are worshipped and used in initiation ceremonies, while no images are used to depict the Supreme Being.

The earliest written accounts of man's religious ideas also suggest a belief in one God who was superior to any other. The Sanskrit *Vedas*, India's earliest literature, give an account of the nomadic Aryan tribes who came to settle in India. The *Vedas* are the hymns which the priests chanted as they presented sacrifice to God. These hymns are uniformly henotheistic in the sense that many names are given to God, but in each case God is seen as the Supreme Being of the universe. It is only in later Vedic literature that henotheism clearly becomes polytheism as the names for God become so personified that they develop into separate gods.

The original Supreme Being of the Aryans was known among all the Indo-European nations. As Robert Brow recounts in his book *Religion: Origins and Ideas*, the first name of this Supreme Being was *Dyaus Pitor* ('Divine Father') which is the same as the Greek *Zeus Pater*, the Latin *Jupiter* or *Deus*, the Early German *Tiu* or *Ziu*, and the Norse *Jyr*. Another name was 'The Heavenly One' (Sanskrit *Varuna*, Greek *Ouranos*), or 'The Friend' (Sanskrit *Mitra*, Persian *Mithra*).

Polytheistic ideas seem to have stemmed from the highly developed cultures of the Middle East, rather than from more primitive societies. There are many similarities in the polytheistic ideas of West African, Egyptian, Mesopotamian and Indo-European regions, while many more primitive peoples are singularly lacking in polytheistic ideas. The religions of E. Asia and of the Andine South America have no polytheism, and China and Japan appear to have received it only through Indian Buddhism.

The anthropologist P. W. Schmidt, who once built up a thriving school of anthropology in Vienna, has gone so far as to claim that anthropological evidence suggests a degenerative evolution from monotheism to polytheism together with totemism, fetishism, animism and magic. There is much to support this idea, but most anthropologists would now agree that there is simply not enough evidence to construct any particular theory of the origin of religion. It should be pointed out that the idea of a Supreme Being is often more vague than a full-blooded monotheistic belief. In the absence of historical records, any attempt to place the development of religious ideas in a certain sequence must arise from applying presuppositions which do not stem from the anthropological data.

What is quite clear is that many different ideas about religion and magic normally exist side by side in the same culture or tribe. Many primitive tribes are animistic, practice magic, and yet at the same time believe in a Supreme Being. No evidence can be found that totemism developed at one place and then spread over the whole world. It is widely spread amongst primitive peoples alongside the belief in a Supreme Being. Similarly those who practice polytheism may well assign special importance to one High God who is more powerful than all the others. No convincing chronological sequence can be extracted from current studies in anthropology, and neither is it likely that any ever could be.

One theory on the origin of religion deserves special attention because it draws not only from evolutionary ideas, but also from attempts to support beliefs about human cultural development by reference to the structure of animal societies.

Freud knew very little about anthropology. What he did know came from the totem theory of Robertson Smith, the views of Darwin, and the works of Frazer such as the *The Golden Bough*. Yet despite the lack in his day of actual field-work carried out on primitive peoples, Freud turned to anthropology and current theories on animal behaviour to attempt a description of the beginnings of culture and religion. His basic ideas are outlined in the much-criticized book called *Totem and Taboo*.

Freud quotes with favour the theories of Atkinson about the organization of human society in the stage when man was still supposed to be more or less an ape-like creature. The gorilla was taken as the model for this stage of human development. Humans were apparently organized into small groups, or tribes, each under the domination of a father who possessed all the females. The sons were driven out or killed as they excited the father's jealousy. One day they banded themselves together, and slew and and devoured the father in a cannibalistic feast. The sons then became filled with contradictory feelings. On the one hand they hated their father, since he was such an obstacle to their craving for power and their sexual desires, but on the other hand they loved and admired him as well. A sense of remorse and guilt began to be felt by the rebellious group, and the dead father became more real than the living one had been. Totems, such as certain animals, were then identified with the father, and a taboo was established against killing them. At the same time, as the sons realized the futility of quarrelling for the daughters, a taboo was established forbidding incest. The memory of the father, who had been both feared and admired, was preserved by the occasional ceremonial killing of the taboo animal, thereby both commemorating and renewing the guilt.

Freud's theory of religion is contained in this allegorical story, for in it he sees the evolution of the memory of the father into the belief in a Father-God who is both loved and feared. It is Freud's thesis in *The Future of an Illusion* that religion is 'the universal obsessional neurosis of humanity' in which is perpetuated the illusion of a loving heavenly Father who promises happiness in the hereafter in return for the renunciation of instinctive desires on earth. In *Moses and Monotheism* Freud attempted to apply similar ideas to the growth of Biblical religion by a series of strange speculations for which there is no historical support.

The detail of Freud's theories has been generally forgotten. But the basic idea that man's belief in God stems from a projection of the father-image is still widely held. Indeed it is actively canvassed as a doctrine of communist propaganda. Since religion, according to Marx, was the 'opium of the people', what could be more like opium than clinging on to the illusion of a father-figure which arises out of a sense of psychological need?

A somewhat simplified adaptation of Freud's ideas appears in Desmond Morris's *The Naked Ape*. In this case the idea of a social group with a dominant overlord is seen occurring at the original ape stage. Dr Morris then postulates that with our immediate ancestors the idea of dominance had to be modified. 'With the growth of the co-operative spirit so vital for successful group hunting, the application of the dominant individual's authority had to be severely limited if he was to retain the active, as opposed to passive, loyalty of the other group leaders.' But the 'change in the order of things, vital as it was to the new social system, nevertheless left a gap. From our ancient background there remained a need for an all-powerful figure who could keep the group under control, and the vacancy was filled by the invention of a god.'

In Dr Morris's book *The Human Zoo* there is even a revival of the old evolutionary ideas about the development of religion, and he confidently states that 'In the smaller and more backward cultures today the minor gods still rule, but members of the major cultures have turned to the single super-god' – despite the fact that no anthropological evidence supports the contention.

It is fascinating the way that certain pseudo-scientific myths become so established in man's mind that their reappearance in varying garbs in each generation may be predicted with near certainty. Clearly there is little or no evidence which could possibly be produced to support Freud's original speculations.

First, Freud's model of gorilla society as the basis for the organizational structure of man's immediate ancestors does not tally with the facts. As Dr Robin Fox points out in a recent issue of the *Journal of the Royal Anthropological Institute*, in a gorilla group there is usually more than one adult male. While there are relations of dominance between the males, there is little aggressiveness or competition. The dominant male is not in fact jealous, and allows females to copulate with other males, and there is no evidence of young males being driven out, since they may leave freely and wander for a time before joining other bands. The same variety and flexibility of organization characterizes other animal societies, as we noted in the last chapter. In chimpanzee societies sexual relations are permissive and there is no sign of a dominant male. Dr Victor Reynolds points out, also in the *Journal of the Royal Anthropological Institute*, that 'a species such as the gibbon, which lives in territorial pairs, cannot be persuaded under any circumstances to form a troop organisation based on a dominant male . . .' Dr Schalles and Dr Emlem conclude in another paper that 'The basic social structure of early hominids may have varied tremendously as a result not only of their mode of life, about which we know a little, but also as a result of their temperament, sex drive and aggression, about which we know nothing.'

Freud's theory about the origin of the totem also finds little support in modern research. It has been shown that the sacrifice and meal of the totem animal is in fact quite rare among peoples which practice totemism. Moreover the Indo-Europeans, Hamito-Semites and Ural-Altaic peoples originally did not appear to have any totemism. Yet it is in just these races that one rarely finds cannibals, and indeed cannibalism is extremely rare amongst the oldest cultures.

When we come to Dr Morris's idea that our 'immediate ancestors' developed a religious system with a god possessing the attributes of a deposed male, then a further problem arises. Since Dr Morris does not define exactly who these 'immediate ancestors' are supposed to be, it is difficult to know who he means. If he means the Australopithecines, who have a brain size of about 600–700 c.c., then it is extremely unlikely that they had the ability to communicate the complex ideas needed for such a religious system. How then was the desire to submit communicated? By making material representations? By telepathy? In fact, as Dr Michael Day shows in his *Guide to Fossil Man*, nothing has been found with the remains of Australopithecines which is as definite as a god, nor appearing with the sort of regularity one would expect from a vital cultural object.

If the details of these theories find little support, then neither does the general concept that religious ideas spring out of a certain type of organization in society. As Professor Evans-Pritchard remarks: 'The supposition that a certain kind of religion goes with, or is the product of, a certain type of social structure, would only have a high degree of probability if it could be shown historically not only that changes in social structure have caused corresponding changes in religious thought, but also that it is a regular correspondence; or if it could be shown that all societies of a certain type have similar religious systems.' In fact it has never been shown that a similar organization of society leads to similar religious systems.

The same arguments apply to the general idea that belief in God stems from the projected need for a father-figure. If the theory be true then one should be able to show that the conceptions of deities vary with the very different roles the father plays in the family in different types of society. It has never been shown that

D

the conceptions of deities vary in this way, and the only prop which could possibly be used to support the idea is therefore removed.

Evans-Pritchard has commented on evolutionary ideas of the origin of religion in general: 'By the time all the exceptions have been registered . . . the remains of the theories are little more than plausible guesses of so general and vague a character that they are of little scientific value, all the more so since nobody knows what to do with them.' It is not therefore the truth or falsity of the biological theory of evolution which concerns us here. All we have tried to show is that if an attempt is made to wrench the idea of evolution out of its biological context and apply it in the realms of ethics and religion, then the end result is most decidedly nonsense.

Words, words, words

Ever since the basic outline of the scientific method was established in the seventeenth century, there has been the temptation to suggest that the kind of information which the method provides is the 'only real truth' about a particular situation. This tendency has come to be known as positivism.

Positivism is particularly connected with the name of the nineteenth-century French philosopher Auguste Comte. It is far more sweeping than the extension of a single scientific model beyond its original context, since it claims that no valid knowledge can ever be known apart from the ideas or things which can be studied by the methods of science. Indeed it was some of the fallacies which arise out of this belief that we were discussing in the last chapter.

In the twentieth century, positivistic ideas have been especially applied in language and the use of words. This stream of thought stems from the views of the British philosopher David Hume, who in the eighteenth century expounded a vigorous scepticism about all statements which did not 'contain any experimental reasoning concerning matter of fact and existence'. Hume's ideas were developed into a full-blooded system of philosophy by a group of philosophers working at the University of Vienna in the 1920s. The group soon became known as the Vienna Circle, and their ideas as Logical Positivism. Their philosophy was popularized in England by Professor A. J. Ayer in a book published in 1936 called *Language, Truth and Logic*.

The central weapon of Logical Positivism was the Verification Principle. According to the Verification Principle the way to find out if a statement is factually meaningful is to ask how it could be verified. If the statement could in principle be verified in such a way that anyone could carry out tests to confirm it, as in science, then it is deemed meaningful and worthwhile. If however no scientific criteria may be put forward to support the statement, then it is rejected as being meaningless. The technique was not therefore concerned with whether something was true, but with whether or not it was meaningful. In this way it could be used to draw a distinction between those questions worth investigating and those which were strictly speaking nonsense. This was like earlier positivistic ideas except that it shifted the emphasis one stage further back, from the validity of factual claims to the validity of the actual words being used to express them.

For instance something could not possibly be 'good' or 'bad' according to the Verification Principle, because this implies a value-judgment which goes a long way beyond the kind of evidence which could be obtained by the scientific method.

No school of philosophy labelled 'Logical Positivism' remains today, though it has greatly influenced the development of British philosophy towards its current concern with linguistic analysis. The downfall of Logical Positivism came with the simple criticism that the Verification Principle itself could not in fact be verified by its own criteria. It was like trying to climb up a ladder and at the same time saw off the rungs just below as you go up. Positivism was shown in fact to be a metaphysical system whereby a value-judgment had been smuggled in to its basic starting-point. Professor Ayer in fact later admitted the validity of the objection, though still holding on to the Verification Principle as a 'convention'.

If the philosophy is taken as a technique for finding out what belongs to strictly scientific discourse, and what belongs to other kinds of discourse, then it certainly has its uses. Muddles often do come from mixing different types of language. But the absurdity comes, as we saw in chapter two, when scientific language is treated as if it were the only language that really mattered. We have also seen that there is no such thing as 'pure objectivity'. Rather there is a continuum between the objective and the subjective. Where linguistic philosophy can help is to keep science as far up the 'objective end' of the continuum as possible.

Once the Verification Principle is applied rigorously, then concepts of art, music, love, God, good, bad, beauty, and a lot of other things beside, are simply assigned as 'meaningless'. Many not unnaturally feel that this is a rather high price to pay for the prior step of assigning value to positivistic assumptions.

This is not to say of course that those philosophers who hold positivistic ideas would allow such ideas to influence their everyday lives. Indeed many have had a rich appreciation of the arts. This underlines one of the sad facts about British philosophy, that it has been relegated in the main to a kind of academic game which is concerned only with words, completely divorced from real life. In the good old days it used to be concerned with the kind of questions and issues which actually faced people in their everyday lives. Now it seems that philosophers deserve the old gag made against theologians, that they can only 'babble and mutter'. It has even been wickedly suggested that the addiction of current philosophy to words and their meanings may represent a kind of mystical escapism from a world of real problems and real questions.

Logical Positivism was perhaps the climax of attempts to make science into a god. Yet from this point of highest exaltation stemmed the greatest reaction against it, a reaction which is busily continuing in the 1970s. Even as Professor Schlick was sharpening up the wits of his group of philosophers in the 'Vienna Circle', so painters were savagely scouring their canvasses with productions that shocked the bourgeois society of their time, and shouting protests against the soulless rationalism which shut them in a box where even their feelings of humanity seemed doomed to everlasting ·impotence. It is the characteristics and extent of this reaction that will concern us in the rest of this chapter.

The flight from reason

We have now surveyed many attempts to justify beliefs by using scientific models quite outside their original scientific context. In each case, as science in this way has been made a god, so it has been seen to be a god that fails. In no case does the evidence allow such extrapolations. This in itself has led many people to realize the limitations of science.

In the twentieth century a much deeper attack on the methods of science has come through a reaction against the very processes of reasoning which are essential for its existence. Scientific method depends on the basic premise of classical logic. If A is A then it cannot be non-A. If a kettle of water boils at 100°C at sea-level, then it cannot also boil at 95°C. Something cannot be red and at the same time be blue.

The early scientists had a world-view in which there were physical and moral absolutes. The basis for all these absolutes was God himself who kept the whole universe in motion and established the laws on which it was based. Since God was a rational God, then it was reasonable to look for order and pattern in the universe which he had created. If an apple fell to the ground one day, then it was just as likely to do the same the next day because gravity was due to the same reasonable God in each case.

The large part that Christianity played in the growth of science has been very well documented. Historians such as Professor Butterfield in *The Origins of Modern Science*, sociologists such as R. K. Merton in *Social Theory and Social Structure* and scientists such as the international symposium which produced *The Scientific Enterprise and Christian Faith* (edited by Malcolm Jeeves) have all shown the deep roots that science has in Christianity. For example of the ten who constituted the original founders of the Royal Society in 1645, only one, Scarborough, was not of Protestant origin. When in 1663 the first full members of the Royal Society were elected, 42 out of 68 were Protestant – far more proportionately than there were Protestants in Britain.

It is significant that science as we know it today began in a Christian European civilization, and nowhere else. This is not to say that it could not have started somewhere else, but the fact remains that it did not. Indeed it is difficult to see how it could have sprung from other world-views, such as Hinduism. If, for example, we accept the strongly monistic positions of the Indian philosopher Shankara, then the only reality is God, and the world itself is *maya*, or imagination. Natural phenomena are therefore like dreams or illusions, and our main aim in life should be to realize the dream-like nature of all that we think and know, and seek to become identified with the Absolute, which is identical with one's deepest self. One attains this by what is called the way of knowledge, and Yoga meditation is one of the paths to attain this realization and unity with the 'ground of all being'. In other words there is no God to impose order on everything. God is the ground of everything, and anything apart from him is illusion. So in trying to practice science there would be no particular reason why one illusion should be any better than another. If ten experiments contradict each other then it does not really matter because it is all a dream anyway. But once there is a God who is separate from, though active in, the universe which he is creating, then there is reason to believe that the universe will show some consistency. As Alfred Whitehead has pointed out in contrasting the European world-view with other civilizations: 'When we compare this tone of thought in Europe with the attitude of other civilizations when left to themselves, there seems but one source for its origin. It must come from the medieval insistence on the rationality of God.'

Science and rationality have always gone hand in hand. Yet as science became more and more successful, so its roots in the Christian world-view began to be forgotten. First, in the deistic view, as we have seen, God was relegated to the position of a

First Cause, the one who started the whole thing off, but who could now be comfortably relegated to the side-lines because science was quite adequate to give a fully satisfactory mechanistic explanation, thank-you-very-much. God was occasionally brought in to explain otherwise inexplicable phenomena, as when Isaac Newton in his great work *Principia Mathematica* (1687) suggested that the paths of comets must be due to a direct intervention of God because they could not be explained by his mathematical formulae. But for all practical purposes God was unnecessary.

In one sense, the early deists were right. If a satisfactory scientific explanation could be found for something, then it was absurd to try to make God into a rival explanation, since after all he was the one who was responsible for the whole process. The eventual mistake of the deists was to make their scientific explanation autonomous and to suggest that the whole cosmic system could be explained by science without reference to God at all.

The next stage was inevitable. If science could explain everything, and God was the distant creator who set the whole system going, then he could be quite readily dispensed with altogether. The rationality derived from a world-view where belief in God was almost universal was kept. But the God himself who had made this rationality possible was discarded. Rationality became rationalism, the theory that man's unaided reason could by itself deal with all man's problems without any recourse to outside help. Man therefore became 'man in the box' (to use Professor H. R. Rookmaaker's phrase) and the world became a closed system where science could in principle give a complete mechanistic description of all phenomena. Man was quite happy to be self-sufficient and to rely only on his own resources.

The seeds of reaction against rationality stem from the moment at which man was put in the box. Little by little over the centuries the significance of what it meant to be in the box became clearer. As scientific descriptions extended to the whole of life, including man himself, in the theory of evolution and in Freud's discovery of the subconscience, so it seemed that the bolts on the box were being tightened. As the mechanisms of life, inheritance and the very workings of our brains are now being unfolded, so it seems to many that the bolts are being driven right home.

At first only a few people realized the full implication of what it meant to rely completely on man's rationality, and go no further than a world-view where man was the measure of all things. The vast majority carried on as before, and even when the belief that man was in a box and there was nothing outside became very strong, many still clung onto the conviction that there were absolutes in life in the realm of standards and morals. It has only really been in this century that the full explosive results of placing man in a closed-system universe have been felt in painting, music, literature and the general culture and life-style of Western man.

David Hume saw the position very clearly in the eighteenth century. In trying to push rationalism to an extreme he questioned the existence of everything, himself included. Yet it is impossible in practice to live out such a thorough-going scepticism. Hume recounts himself how when his very rationality faced him with despair he found an answer in nature which 'cures me of this philosophical melancholy and delirium, either by relaxing this bent of mind, or by some avocation and lively impression of my senses, which obliterate all these chimeras. I dine, I play a game of backgammon, I converse, and am merry with my friends, and when, after three or four hours' amusement, I would return to those speculations, they appear so cold, and strained and ridiculous, that I cannot find it in my heart to enter into them any further.'

Hume's answer was therefore to revel in his own humanity and use this as an escape from the logic of his own conclusions. The Danish philosopher Kierkegaard in the nineteenth century dealt with similar problems in a rather different way. He realized fully the limits of reason, and had a profound belief in God. For Kierkegaard the 'way out of the box' was by a gigantic 'leap of faith', not in itself rational, whereby true knowledge of God could be found. As he wrote in his *Journals*: 'The only salvation is subjectivity, i.e. God, as infinite compelling subjectivity.' Kierkegaard was reacting against the dry metaphysical speculations of men such as Hegel. In his own day his ideas received opposition right to the grave, though now Kierkegaard is seen as a key figure in the growth of modern Existentialism.

Nietzsche in the nineteenth century realized with an awful solemnity exactly what it meant for man to be completely alone in the universe. If many were happy to cling on to their old bourgeois morals, even though their world-view was inexorably changing, Nietzsche understood that if 'God is dead' then all the old Christian values and morals must be dead as well. The only logical result could be nihilism, the belief that nothing remains. As Nietzsche himself wrote: 'What is nihilism? The fact that the highest values lose all value. There is no aim, no answer to the question "Why?" Man has lost all dignity in his own eyes.'

For Nietzsche the answer lay in the deification of man, with his resultant idea of the 'superman' who was to be an affirmation of man's strength, a kind of James Bond passionately committed to lavishness in both good and evil. Yet for Nietzsche himself the results of his life were tragically the opposite. After a life of loneliness, ill health and insomnia there came a day when he saw a horse being flogged by a coachman in Turin. Throwing his arms round it, Nietzsche called the horse his brother and burst into tears. A few days later he broke down insane and remained so for a further ten years until his death in 1900. One crucial fact was present in the life of Nietzsche, if it was absent from his philosophy as taught, that in the dictum 'God is dead' also lies the seeds of the death of man himself. Otherwise Nietzsche is perhaps one of the only prophets of the nineteenth century whose predictions have nearly all come true.

If Nietzsche's life spoke as much as his literature, then a hunt through the private letters and journals of much quieter men may reveal the problems posed by rationalism just as clearly. The letters of Charles Darwin show an interesting progression of thought as old age approached. It is clear that at many points

Darwin found that his humanity seemed to be at stake, and several times expressed puzzlement that his earlier love for music had completely disappeared. Indeed at one time he wrote with regret that 'My mind seems to have become a kind of machine.' At another period of his life he was plagued with doubts as to whether there could be any good reason for supposing that his thoughts had any more value than a monkey's. Darwin was comforted by the not very convincing feeling that he could at least think about the problem, whereas the monkey presumably could not.

In the twentieth century the most powerful reaction against positivism as far as philosophy is concerned has come through the atheistic Existentialism of Jean-Paul Sartre. The roots of this Existentialism are found in Kierkegaard and Nietzsche. Sartre quotes with approval the words of Dostoievsky, 'If God did not exist, everything would be possible.' Sartre views the absence of God as a basic axiom rather than with the sense of dread which filled Nietzsche. The datum of life is that we exist. That is all. Man is very thoroughly in the box. There are no morals or absolutes. 'Man's existence,' says Sartre, 'precedes his essence.' In other words, even before man begins to look at the world and think about what it all means, he must already exist. That must come first. No determinism exists, for by natural definition 'man *is* freedom'. There is only one matter in which he is not free and that is in his freedom. Man was born free, he did not choose to become free, so he is condemned to be free. According to Sartre this means that man has total responsibility. He chooses everything that happens. If he chooses not to act then that too is a choice.

Sartre sees the 'way out of the box' in a similar way to Kierkegaard, only without God. For Sartre man is God. He must authenticate himself by his own decisions, he must find his humanity in his own leaps of faith. He must act decisively. Since God is dead, and therefore morals are dead, there is no such thing as a 'right' decision or a 'wrong' decision. The importance lies in the fact that a decision is taken, and in how it is taken. The authentic man is one who accepts his God-like responsibilities seriously, in anguish, rather than fleeing from them into various forms of self-deception.

'Hell is other people,' wrote Sartre, and by this he meant that the existence of other people must mean a threat to my own subjective freedom. Other people deprive me of my true dignity by treating me as an object, as an 'it' rather than an 'I'. The ultimate deprivation of freedom is death, since in death the play of life ceases to be a melodrama, and becomes a senseless tragedy. 'It is a tragic drama,' writes Walter Odajnyk, 'in which man is the star as well as the director and the author; the beginning is tragic since he is coerced to act his part regardless of his wishes; the middle is tragic since he knows that his past and present actions are but a meaningless prelude to the finale – which is death; and so the end is tragic since what once was a being has now become a void. And somewhere during the process man is asked to face this situation with courage, consider himself free, and even make an attempt at happiness.'

At the heart of Existentialism is a declaration of independence, and at the heart of that independence is a declaration of irrationality. Despite the fact that there is no ultimate meaning in the universe, no ethics and no purpose, man must make a blind leap into declaring his humanity, even though he knows that his life is destined to the final absurdity of death. Life is absurd, but let us practice our freedom faithfully and pretend it is not absurd. This is the anti-rationalism of Existentialism.

Today Existentialism as a systematic philosophy hardly exists, and in France the intellectual prestige of men like Sartre has given place to other thinkers, such as the anthropologist Levi-Strauss. Yet the pervasive attitudes of Existentialism have left a permanent dent on the rigidity of positivism, and though in Britain it never had a great impact as a philosophy, its influence has been powerfully felt in literature, drama and music.

If Existentialism represents one of the most systematic twentieth-century flights from rationalism, then there are plenty of other examples which are more mundane, but nevertheless just as real. One of the characteristics of the move away from rationalism is that it touches all kinds of people in every walk of life, sometimes when they least expect it, and often when they do not even realize it.

In the nineteenth century it was much easier to exist as 'man in the box' because most people were still optimistic, and the pleasurable feeling that man was going somewhere was sufficient compensation for any facts which suggested otherwise. Many still held that some kind of moral absolutes could improve society and help to give it cohesion. Yet, as we have seen, this cosy picture has been shattered by the events of the twentieth century, and it seems now that there is no particular reason for believing that man is going anywhere. One of the irrationalities of modern man is to hold onto optimistically progressive views of human nature in the teeth of all the evidence which suggests otherwise. As the Cambridge astronomer Professor Fred Hoyle writes in *The Nature of the Universe:* 'Only the biological processes of mutation and natural selection are needed to produce living creatures as we know them. Such creatures are no more than ingenious machines that have evolved as strange by-products in an odd corner of the Universe . . . Most people object to this argument for the not very good reason that they do not like to think of themselves as machines . . . Here we are in this wholly fantastic Universe with scarcely a clue as to whether our existence has any real significance.'

Henry Miller, at one time Professor of Neurology at Newcastle University, and now its Vice-Chancellor, put the situation in a nutshell when he stated in a radio broadcast that 'Although scientific materialism is an unfashionable philosophy, and an optimistic materialism even more out of tune with the cultural pessimism that is so popular today, it is, in fact, the philosophical basis on which most of us organize our lives.' In other words many will carry on clinging to the idea that man has some kind of meaning or value even when the very box that he has put himself in suggests that everything is meaningless anyway. The only way out is by an irrational affirmation that man does have meaning and purpose because he feels that way, rather than there being any particular reason for having them.

A classic example of this irrationality was seen recently in a speech given to the Rationalist Press Association by Professor H. Gwynne Jones, Professor of Psychology at Leeds University. 'We seek a freedom,' said Professor Jones, 'which is limited only by allowing the same freedom to others and of course by such factors as distress, disease and suffering and so on. In fact this sort of society would mobilize its resources maximally to combat these evils. But in saying that kind of thing, I think that one also implies a belief, or more than a belief, a hope in the essential goodness of human nature. That I think is not rationally based at all and in fact is belied by most of the evidence in the world today. Nevertheless, I do believe it.' The enormousness of this leap of faith leaves one gasping, more especially when stated in the context of a society which claims rationality as its very foundation-stone.

Dr Francis Schaeffer recounts in his book *Escape from Reason* how Professor Anthony Flew once ran into a similar type of problem when giving a broadcast talk under the title 'Must Morality Pay?' Professor Flew came to the conclusion that, according to his own assumptions, the answer was 'no', morality does not pay. Yet so strong was the feeling to hang on to a bourgeois morality, that right at the end of the programme he brought out of thin air the concept that, in spite of the fact that morality does not pay, a man is not a fool to be scrupulous.

Similar 'leaps of faith' can be seen in the views of Sir Julian Huxley, which we have already discussed. In *The Essays of a Humanist* Huxley proposed the new 'religion of fulfilment' which would provide 'bustling secular man' with experience of the 'deeper and higher aspects of existence'. The humanist religion would have to 'work out its own rituals and its own basic symbolism.' Huxley has even gone so far as to speak of a worshipful new Trinity which he describes as the powers of nature, the ideal goals of the human mind, and actual human beings in so far as they embody the human ideals. It is unlikely in the extreme that any such religion will catch on, any more than did the similar ideas of Auguste Comte in the last century. What is significant is that in the name of a supposedly rational humanism Huxley is suggesting that man needs a religion even though that religion is not true. In other words, because society has a psychological need for a religion, then it should believe a lie to satisfy a need. This would seem to be the worst kind of opium of the people.

The ideals of a kind of cosmic optimism have been kept alive in a very different way in the tenets of Marxist-Leninism. Communism has often been compared to a religious system. Indeed the Swiss scholar Professor Arnold Kuezli maintains that the communist revolution is far from the scientific inevitability that Marx suggested. Rather it is an apocalyptic vision of the Second Coming with the individual, personal Messiah removed and a Hegelian intellectual abstraction put in his place. In this way the Christian belief that history was going somewhere could be kept alive. Professor Kuezli's psychological interpretation of Marx has hardly had a warm reception from communists, though his views are supported by the observation that Marx and his followers only had the vaguest ideas of what should be done after the Revolution (because the Messiah will take care of everything), and also by the historical fact that Marxism seems to flourish in the midst of nominal Christianity. For example, the state of Kerala in India has the highest proportion of nominal Christians of any Indian state, and at the same time one of the highest proportions of communists. Since one characteristic of nominal Christianity is the rejection of a hope in a real second coming of Christ, so Kuezli suggests that the need for that hope is kept alive by embracing Marxism.

In a more general way communism certainly seems to show all the essential characteristics of a religion. Of prophets there are plenty, both living and dead, whether it be Lenin in the Mausoleum in Moscow, Dimitrov in Sofia, or Mao in China. The devil has now become Western imperialism and capitalism, and the inflamed enthusiasm of China's millions is daily kept alive against these 'paper tigers' and 'running dogs'. The dangers of liberalism within the ranks is represented by revisionism, the watering down of the pure doctrine of the prophet Marx, to whom the original revelation was given. Martyrs are revered with religious fervour. In Cuba the martyrdom and eventual deification of Che Guevara was enough to rekindle the ebbing courage of a starving nation where the leaders had not been able to keep their promises, and in China much is still made of the approximately one million men who died in the Korean War. Their stories are well known, and many towns have their own heroes.

It is in China that communism most closely approaches a religious system. Pilgrims stream to Mao's birthplace at Shaoshan in Hunan. Mao's thoughts are discussed, applied, memorized and poured out through a complex propaganda machine twenty-four hours a day. From postage stamps to railway engines quotations from Chairman Mao bombard the people. 'Chairman Mao is the red sun in our hearts, his thoughts shed light over the world.' Group sharing and criticism are a normal part of the daily programme. Beneath it all is one basic conviction – that the progress of Mao's revolution is inevitable and there is a great future ahead.

The idea of a future New Age has cropped up repeatedly in human history. Imperial Russia looked upon Moscow as the third and final Rome. The Third Reich of Adolf Hitler, seen as a successor to the Holy Roman and Bismarckian Empires, was in a sense a mystical vision of a new messianic Third Age. All Utopian political or social visions have tended to embody this kind of political messianism.

In a book published in 1970 called *The Greening of America*, Professor Charles Reich of Yale University paints his vision of a new world order which will arise out of a change in consciousness. Consciousness 1, says Professor Reich, was represented by the small-town, largely Christian, traditional values. Consciousness 2 is characterized by materialistic, liberal and progress-orientated values. The culminating stage is consciousness 3 where man will experience the final liberating age of spiritual freedom and maturity.

All such dreams of progress are essentially mystical in content, because they all depend on a blind faith in the future which is not justified by the facts of the present. Whether it is Huxley's new religion, Marx's future messianic communist society, or Reich's consciousness 3, the same anti-rationality is present, because there is little evidence to suggest that any of these future states will actually take place.

Scientists themselves have not very often realized the full implication of what it means to be 'man in the box'. This has partly been due to the fact that the majority of scientists have been drawn from the middle classes, and have therefore clung onto a bourgeois mentality and sought to maintain the status quo. Indeed a bourgeois mentality is essential for carrying out science itself. Scientific research depends on the rules of truthfulness, honesty, hard work, group co-operation and effective communication. For the early scientists of course these qualities sprang naturally from their Christian belief. These morals were seen as absolutes which depended on the Absolute, God himself. As the idea of God went, so the idea of absolute morals went with him. But the scientist is not particularly worried, because his method of working is essentially pragmatic. If something works then it must be true. Bourgeois morals work, so that is a good enough reason for keeping them.

As the reaction against science and the rationalism which underlies it has continued, so many scientists have become increasingly schizophrenic in their intellectual thinking. In the laboratory reason reigns supreme, because that is the only way that science can continue, but in everyday life many younger scientists are adopting the experience-seeking life-styles which are modern man's way of getting out of the box of machinery into which rationalism seems to have put him.

Some, in the past, have found a reinforcement of their feelings of humanity in the very process of discovery itself. The scientist-novelist C. P. Snow tells of the unique experience which overcame him when a scientific prediction was verified after a series of failures: 'Then I was carried beyond pleasure . . . My own triumph and delight and success were there, but they seemed insignificant beside this tranquil ecstasy . . . I had never known that such a moment could exist . . . Since then I have never quite regained it. But one effect will stay with me as long as I live; once, when I was young, I used to sneer at the mystics who have described the experience of being at one with God and part of the unity of things. After that afternoon, I did not want to laugh again, for though I should have interpreted the experience differently, I thought I knew what it meant.' Others in the history of science have shared similar experiences. Pasteur wrote: 'When you have at last arrived at certainty, your joy is one of the greatest that can ever be felt by a human soul.' Scheele, the discoverer of chlorine, exclaimed: 'Oh, how happy I am . . . there is no delight like that which comes from discovery.' When the chemist Davy saw the alkali metals floating like silver balls in his molten mixture, he is said to have literally danced for joy.

Such human experiences have come through the practice of science itself. But no scientist could ever account for such experiences within the limits of the scientific method. Man's experiences of joy, love, hate, peace, beauty or exaltation have no significance in it. Immediately one accepts that man is in a closed system of matter and chance and time, but nothing more, then there is no real reason for thinking that his mechanics have any more significance than the bouncing of a ball on a ping-pong table. Professor J. B. S. Haldane put the point very succinctly when he said: 'If all my thoughts are due to the behaviour of electrical changes within my brain, like the behaviour of billiard balls on a table is due to the direction in which they are struck, then how can I have any thoughts which are valid about my brain; how do I know that truth exists . . .'

The strong twentieth-century reaction against the dry rational-ism of science has been recently surveyed by Theodore Roszak, Professor of History at the California State College, and author of *The Making of a Counter Culture*. In a recent article in *Humanist* magazine entitled 'Ecology and Mysticism' he states: 'I think the most potentially important aspect of this disaffiliation arises where the counter culture begins to diverge markedly from something that has not been very seriously questioned in the mainstream of Western society for a few hundred years at least, and that is the scientific and technological tradition of our culture. This is the tradition we have long understood to represent "Progress", "Reason" and human dignity. I think I'm right in saying that the significance of the increasing interest in drugs, oriental religions, mysticism, the occult, and in a great deal of what is now called in the US "affective education", or the "human potentials movement" . . . does represent a radical departure from scientific orthodoxy.' Professor Roszak suggests that one day we might have 'a new science in which the object of knowledge will be rather like the poet's beloved; something to be contemplated but not analyzed, something that is permitted to retain its mysteries.'

Not surprisingly Roszak's ideas have produced a strong reaction from more traditional humanists, such as Edmund Leach, who feel that the very foundations of humanism are at stake. Indeed their feelings are quite correct. The principles of humanism are at stake. But what is truly doubtful is whether the principles of humanism can possibly survive the onslaughts which are being made on them as we move towards the end of the twentieth century.

Man has clung on to many beliefs which have helped him to believe that life 'in the box' is not so meaningless and pointless as his reason might suggest. For some it has been a blind optimism or political idealism, for others it has been an existential commitment to life, for the majority perhaps it has been a grim determination not to be troubled by ultimate questions. But undoubtedly for millions of people it has been the adoption of life-styles which have placed more emphasis on experience and subjectivity than on logic and reason.

The most obvious example of the deliberate adoption of an alternative life-style was in the beatnik and hippie movements. When the town council in Venice, California, was about to close down a particularly notorious beatnik cafe, a lady asked to testify before them, presumably to clinch the case against the offenders. When, however, she came to give evidence, it was to say that each day as she walked past the cafe it was full of 'unsavoury types' who were 'just standing there, looking nonchalant'. This seemingly uncondemning description is very significant because it sums up their crime against her world-view. In the world of science and technology if something happens, then something else happens as a result. In the world of beat philosophy things just are, and that's all, and 'cool' and 'nonchalant' are the essence of their life-style.

Aldous Huxley is in many ways the most important prophet of modern mysticism, and already in the early fifties he was exploring the 'antipodes of the mind' with psychedelic drugs. But it was not until the pushing of mind-expanding drugs such as LSD by Timothy Leary, Allan Ginsberg and Ken Kesey that the acid-trip really caught on. The infatuation with LSD was accompanied by a new interest in marijuana, a drug with which the beats had long experimented.

It was in January 1959 that Dr Tim Leary, a convert from Irish Roman Catholicism to Hinduism, entered the 'Centre of Research on the Personality' at Harvard. In August 1960 Dr Leary spent his summer vacation sampling Mexican mushrooms which he had heard about from Aldous Huxley. In January 1961 a symposium entitled 'The Control of the Human Mind' was held at the University of California with 26 scientists and writers. Huxley re-affirmed his view that 'certain drugs can develop and expand the limits of human thought'. Soon afterwards Huxley met Leary and they decided to unite their efforts. In the early sixties Leary and his disciples experimented with LSD and other drugs at Harvard. By the time Leary was expelled from Harvard in 1963 (despite the intervention of Huxley, who died later in the same year) the use of LSD was widespread.

From the start it was largely among the bourgeois middle-classes that LSD use was most common. As Dr Richard Blum reported in 1964: 'It is a phenomenon concentrated among respected, conforming, successful persons with socially favoured backgrounds and careers.' In other words it was just those whose roots were deepest in the success of a technological society who felt the greatest need for a leap into transcendence. The affirmation of humanity through a mystical experience came from those who realized most vividly what it meant to be 'man in the box'. From the beginning LSD-use was closely linked with a search for spirituality, a quest for Nirvana and the attempt to find true meaning in life. After being thrown out of Harvard, Leary published *The Psychedelic Experience* (which was adapted from the *Tibetan Book of the Dead*) and *Psychedelic Prayers* (which followed a sacred Chinese book called the *Tao Te King*).

At the heart of the acid-trip was the exaltation of irrationality. It was a release from sanity to madness by destroying the inner restrictive order which had somehow survived the dissolution of the outer. The schizophrenic replaced the sage as the new ideal, and in Ken Kesey's *One Flew Over the Cuckoo's Nest* the new culture hero is pictured as a giant schizoid Indian whose madness is modelled in part on the author's experiences with LSD.

The rise and fall of the hippie movement has already been well documented. Its demise resulted partly from its very size. It is not much fun dropping out of a pointless bourgeois life-style when everyone else is doing the same. Protest is essentially a minority activity. Also the effects of LSD were not as rosy as earlier prophecies had made out. Too many people were having 'bum' trips. In the eighteen months prior to March 1967, no less than 130 users of LSD had been under psychiatric treatment at one American hospital – the Bellevue Hospital in Washington. Early in 1966 Stephen Kessler, an ex-medical student, was arrested in Brooklyn for cutting the throat of his mother-in-law with a kitchen knife. He had been high on LSD for three days. Soon there were cases of car accidents and attempted flights from high buildings by those under the influence of acid.

Even when the trip was a good one there was always the annoying experience of having to come back to earth again and live in a real world. One regular LSD-user put it like this: 'What I really dig is art and music and poetry. But every time I have to study for exams I quit taking drugs almost entirely. I see the dirty job of getting through school as incompatible with the view of life that comes through taking drugs. That view, well, more ecstasy in life, is open, spontaneously creative, sensual . . . Ordinary people become like gods and goddesses.'

As underground newspapers started warning followers against getting too involved with 'tripsters', so there was also some disenchantment with communal living. There was the disquieting discovery that the evils of bourgeois society seemed to crop up in miniature even in a community where everything was shared in common. Sometimes problems came over the most mundane questions, such as which member of the group was going to make the main decisions. The problem for the hippie was neatly summed up in the words of Dostoievsky: 'Abstract love of humanity is nearly always egoism.'

The quest for spiritual experience continues unabated. In the great majority of cases the search is being made in non-rational directions. There is the continued revival of interest in Eastern religions, non-theistic forms of meditation, chanting of mantras, beat Zen as well as square Zen, Yoga, and so on. Meher Baba, Gandalf the White Wizard, and a host of Zen Buddhist teachers, yogis and gurus can all claim disciples from among what Dr Allan Cohen has called 'metahippies'. Dr Cohen's progression from being a follower of Tim Leary to the search for non-chemical approaches to consciousness is typical of the path many have taken.

Together with the emphasis on eastern religions there has been a striking growth of occult and magical movements and a multiplication of esoteric sects. One occultist order – the Hemetic Order of the Golden Dawn – which flourished a century ago in Britain and was thought to be extinct, has now reappeared. Police files are full of the activities of latter-day witches, including celebrations of the 'Black Mass'. There has been a major revival of astrology, mystical ideas about the 'Age of Aquarius' and the 'Glastonbury Zodiac'. Astrology is big business. In February 1971 a college lecturer in Leeds revealed that he was using the stars for family planning, calculating the best times for the birth of his projected family!

However the greatest and most popular quest for an experience which will lead modern man beyond his seeming trap in a mechanistic universe has come through the deification of sex. The sex experience itself has seemed for many the way out of the box. It seems to have all the advantages of ready availability, transcendental quality and the fact that in expressing man's most human emotions there is strong feeling of some kind of meaning which lies above and beyond the purely mechanistic. Even though reason seems to dictate that sex is finally just a complex chemical and psychological phenomenon which produces certain transient mechanical changes in the body, the experience seems to suggest, or perhaps gives the illusion, that there is something much more. As Simon and Garfunkel put it:

> 'And so you see I have come to doubt
> All that I once held as true;
> I stand alone without beliefs,
> The only truth I know is you.'

Some might feel that Camus' hero Mersault in *The Outsider* was being more honest when, after wrestling with the concept of love in the light of total meaninglessness, he ends up by having to do away with it altogether. In one of Sartre's stories the lover holds the girl's hand as she lies in bed. There is contentment until suddenly the full weight of what it means to be a physical object bears down upon him, and as he imagines the same hand cut off and lying on the operating table he asks: 'How can I love an object which might make me disgusted?'

The problem with trying to get out of 'the box' by mystical, drug or sex experience is that the experience does not last very long. At the end there is the same sense of hollowness as a landing is made back into the familiar world of three dimensions. As Paul Simon expresses it in his song *America:*

> 'Kathy, I'm lost,' I said,
> Though I knew she was sleeping.
> 'I'm empty and aching and I don't know why.'

As soon as the sex experience, for example, becomes something done for its own sake, divorced from a permanent relationship, then there is the strange sensation of its merging into meaninglessness. It becomes a temporary leap into would-be ecstasy which, like the sighing of the wind in the trees, is soon swallowed up by the passing of time.

There is also the uncomfortable fact that the human body is not a machine for generating experiences ad infinitum without, at least, some considerable psychological and mental wear and tear. For drug-users it may come through bad trips or more long-term effects which may warrant extensive psychiatric care. As Johnny Cash put it bluntly: 'When you take drugs you may be in ecstasy for a few minutes, but you're soon on the ridge of terror. Take it from a guy who's been there: it ain't worth it.' For the worshipper of free sex it may come through venereal disease (increasingly so, as figures released in Britain in February 1972 showed only too clearly), or in unwanted pregnancies with subsequent abortions, together with the unhappy experiences which cause problems in adjusting to the sex-life of later marriage.

But sexual anarchy has long been coupled with political revolution as a symbolic protest against traditional values. The Communist Party Manifesto of the last century glibly proclaimed that 'of course the bourgeois family will disappear with the disappearance of its complements . . .' Yet after the 1917 revolution in Russia an attempt to liberalize laws to give complete sexual freedom led to bands of illegitimate children roaming the countryside, and the experiment was soon halted. Today the sexual climate of Russian society is staid compared with the permissiveness of the West. But sexual liberation is still equated with political liberation, and in Russia's dissident intellectual 'underground' the declaration of freedom against a repressive state is symbolized in illegal magazines such as *Mtsyry* in which a super-woman called Octobriana stalks the pages with well-endowed proportions, protecting minority groups as she goes.

The student protest of the 1960s was very much a symptom of the youthful disaffection with a society which seemed intent on the building of university factories geared to the production of pre-packaged academic success. Among other things it was a reaction against the very nature of man which the universities themselves were seeking to impose – that bourgeois version of Humanism with its view of man as justified by rationality, work, duty, vocation, maturity and success.

As the explosions of May 1968 in France sent ripples across the world's universities, so for many the explosions were a savagely cynical indictment of the precepts of Rousseau so faithfully served up in the philosophical curricula of French secondary schools. If the kind of reason that Rousseau emulated resulted in that kind of society, then so much the worse for reason. In the anarchistic wing of student politics all the old apostles of reason are decried, Freud as much as Socrates. The old Socratic adage that the unexamined life is not worth living is rejected for precisely the reason that the unexamined life is the only one worth enduring at all. In the brief but well-publicized 'Dirty Speech Movement' which took place on the Berkeley campus of the University of California, the streams of sexual liberation and anti-rationalism met in an assault on language itself, the ultimate anti-word.

'We have all heard of the march of science,' wrote Charles Lamb, 'but who shall beat the drums of its retreat?' It now seems that the retreat is coming through a thorough-going disassociation from the very principles of reason which have made the scientific method possible.

The machinery of science and technology marches on. Within its framework the old culture is retained. Yet the very logic and rationalism of its system has forced the creation of a counter-culture. As man has been pushed towards the chasm of his own meaningless existence, so he has been forced to cry out against the seeming absurdity of the heavens, and reinstate his humanity through a new kind of mysticism. How this has been expressed in contemporary art and literature has been well shown by others (notably Professor H. R. Rookmaaker in *Modern Art and the Death of a Culture*).

The cultural gap itself was symbolized by a high-level Nobel Symposium entitled 'The Place of Values in a World of Facts' which met in Stockholm during September 1970. A bevy of scientist-professors met to try to thrash out a new system of values for a world where the old ones seemed to have been undermined by the very science they had been practising. Their deliberations, needless to say, met with little success. Outside, a group of beat-hippie protesters wrote their own document on the conference: 'To superminds with love', said its title page, 'We do not trust you and we are not grateful. You've never stood up successfully against the military. And then we are crowded in sprawling, soulless cities, having things done to us. We cannot describe exactly what the things are, but we know that you have not come to our aid yet.' It was expressed in blank verse.

The culture and the counter-culture. Are we destined to live in either one or the other? Or must we be condemned for ever to a schizophrenic existence where half our life is lived in a world which may be rational and scientific but which denies our humanity, the other half in a would-be world of restored humanity but without purpose, or meaning, or reason?

Or is there another answer?

Chapter Four

BACK TO SQUARE ONE

Science is rather like the game where you hit a ball attached to a length of elastic. The harder you hit the ball, the further the elastic stretches, and the further the elastic stretches, the more vicious is the rebound. One way the scientific ball is bouncing back into the face of the players today is through the kind of experiments we outlined in chapter one. The new advances are reminding us that the chances of the misuse of science by society are just the same as ever, and that the whole relevance of a relativistic morality is being called into question by the new possibilities of altering man's very physical structure.

When attempts are made to bounce the ball into courts where it does not belong, then the elastic is just not long enough. Scientific models out of context are, to change the analogy, like fish out of water – they will only create confusion until thrown back into the environment where they belong, as we saw in chapters two and three.

Finally, in the modern drift towards mysticism, it seems that the ball is in danger of coming right off the elastic altogether, making the scientific game itself impossible.

Many in the face of such paradoxes simply give up asking questions. Their argument goes something like this. Philosophers have argued for hundreds of years about such great themes as Being, Reality, Meaning and Morals, and they have never been able to come to any conclusions. No sooner was one system erected by one philosopher than it was systematically destroyed by another. The end result is the situation we have today where philosophers have given up asking any real questions at all and contented themselves with the study of words instead. So if such super-minds have failed, what hope have we of doing any better?

The only answer is to pretend there are no questions, and to bury nagging inner voices in the search for pleasure. In fact the central thrust of the mass media today seems to be the over-whelming message that man was made for pleasure and pleasure was made for man. Whether in the extra packet of cigarettes, the extra fat cigar, the plush house and garden, the long cool draught of you-know-what, the result is the same – that titillation of the senses which produces the needed escape. Some leave the television on for as long as the programming hours will allow; even though they are not consciously looking at the screen the constant flicker is a comforting antidote against intruding questions which break through into the mind during times of loneliness. For many the constant blare from a radio or record-player can sufficiently 'blow the mind' to stop it thinking.

Yet the final result of the search for pleasure is nearly always the same – boredom. Recently across the walls of the University of Birmingham library, painted in bold black letters, appeared the words 'APATHY RULES'. Ralph Barton, a former top cartoonist, put it this way: 'I have had few difficulties, many friends, great successes; I have gone from wife to wife, and from house to house, visited great countries of the world, but I am fed up with inventing devices to fill up 24 hours of the day.' The result is a society where, as Henry Thoreau put it, 'Most men live lives of quiet desperation.'

Happily there are many who do in fact still want to think and carry on asking questions. Very often the real questions today are being asked right outside the old academic frameworks. They are being asked in painting and poetry, in literature, folk and pop music. They are being asked by the 'beat-hippie crowd of conceptual illiterates', as one scathing commentator called them, and by thousands of young people who are sick to death of trite, bureaucratic answers. The President of Colombia University has estimated that as many as 50 per cent of students today belong to an 'alienated culture, hostile to science and technology'.

There were four basic questions being asked by the hippie

movement. What is the ultimate power which animates the universe? What is life; when did it commence and where is it going? What is man, his origin and destiny? Who am I, what is my place in the cosmos? The very questions long discarded by philosophers as being meaningless are just the questions which press to be answered in the real world where people live, eat, drink, suffer, die and have children.

How do we go about tackling such questions at all?

More on models

A clue may perhaps be found in the methods of science itself. We have seen that far from having some mystical air of finality, science is rather a search for models that succeed in linking together different phenomena. How persuasive the model is depends on how closely it fits the observed facts, and to what extent it is testable by measurement.

In an analogous way we might test the various 'models' which are being thrown up today to give answers to some of the dilemmas in which modern man finds himself. However, in this case the kinds of facts that we allow as evidence for the model are by no means restricted to scientific data, but rather cover the whole range of human experience. The data are therefore taken from the whole of reality, including history, politics, art, current affairs, films, music, our homes and family life, the whole gamut of our personal experience from birth to whatever age we might be.

The crucial questions to ask are therefore these: Does solution X fit the facts? Is it the kind of model which hangs together and makes sense in the light of my total experience? Has it already been tested in perhaps a different guise by human experience in the past? If so, did it work? If not, is it in principle testable in the crucible of human experience? The method is therefore open-ended. It is willing to adapt as new evidence becomes available. It keeps the open spirit of science, while leaving aside science's strict methodology and interest in only those things which may be measured.

Using these criteria, let us therefore try 'shopping around' for some of the models which are suggested today as answers to man's problems.

One recurring suggestion has to do with the specific problems which are being posed by science itself. The idea here is that since scientists are the ones who understand most about the kind of problems that they are creating, then more power should be handed over from the politicians to groups of scientists chosen for their superior knowledge and wisdom.

So Isaac Asimov writes in a recent guest editorial for *Chemical and Engineering News:* 'And who on earth is most likely to rise above the limitations of national and ethnic prejudice and speak in the name of mankind as a whole? As a class, scientists, I should think. The nations of the world are divided in culture, in language, in religion, in tastes, in philosophy, in heritage – but wherever science exists at all, it is the same science; and scientists from everywhere and anywhere speak the same language, profession-ally, and accept the same mode of thought. Is it not then, as a class, the scientists to whom we must turn to find leaders in the fight for world government?'

A similar thought, put in a more melodramatic way, comes in Robin Clarke's *Science of War and Peace.* 'We are all waiting,' says Clarke, 'for the scientific Luther who will nail his thesis to the laboratory door, carrying a message of equal relevance to capitalist and communist, developed and undeveloped, to the East and West, the North and South.'

This same kind of rather naive elitism has cropped up in a number of recent scientific conferences – for example in the 1970 Nobel Symposium on 'The Place of Values in a World of Facts' which we have already mentioned, and in the 1971 conference of 200 scientists on 'Science and Society' organized by the Weitz-mann Institute. It is also seen in a collection of essays by leading scientists called *The Social Responsibility of the Scientists,* where one gets the impression that if only the 'leading scientists' were consulted in time, then most of the problems would disappear.

A rather more threatening suggestion on a slightly different tack is that made by Dr Paul Ehrlich, author of the best-selling book *The Population Bomb*, when he proposes for the future a 'Department of Population and Environment' in which scientists would play a major role. This department should be given 'broad powers to maintain the quality of life'. These 'broad powers' would include such things as imposing heavy penalties on the misuses of science, massive advertising to reduce the size of the family, the rationing of power, and the introduction of 'laws strictly limiting the number of appliances a single family may possess'. This rather Orwellian picture of DPE men coming to the house to take away the extra child or TV set is hardly an attractive one.

In Professor B. F. Skinner's classic piece of science-fiction called *Walden Two*, the scientist's chief role in society becomes that of the behavioural engineer, the one who conditions the social life of the community by means of psychological conditioning. 'Give me the specification,' says Frazier, the book's hero, amidst the gentle peacefulness of life in 'Walden Two', 'and I'll give you the man.' And as he further points out: 'When a science of behaviour has once been achieved there's no alternative to a planned society. We can't leave mankind to an accidental biased control. But by using the principles of positive reinforcement – carefully avoiding force or the threat of force – we can preserve a personal sense of freedom.' In other words – give the scientist the power and let him get on with the job. The message is the same. But who is going to manipulate the manipulators?

What happens when we start applying the tests suggested above to these kinds of pragmatic models? The first observation, despite Isaac Asimov's remarks, is that there seems to be little agreement amongst scientists on basic moral issues, any more than there is amongst politicians. If proof be needed, it should suffice to glance at the kind of meandering debates about ethics which seem to have become the norm at top-level scientific conferences. A typical example was the Ciba symposium entitled 'Man and his Future', held some years ago, when twenty-seven distinguished scientists grappled with ethical principles. The differences between the moral positions of even this limited number were enormous.

When it comes to the extent to which current lines of research should be allowed to continue, then agreement amongst top scientists is no more united. A current example are the attacks being made on Dr Robert Edwards' research on reproduction at Cambridge by the two Nobel prize-winners Dr James Watson and Dr Max Perutz.

Neither is there any real evidence that scientists would make any less of a mess of 'world leadership' than have politicians. As Henry Miller once put it in a broadcast talk, with tongue slightly in cheek: 'It is tempting to wonder whether some of our problems might be met by replacing unsuccessful statesmen with successful scientists. But the honest materialist must admit to his suspicion that the difficulties of the politician and the triumphs of the scientist reflect the relative intractabilities of their materials rather than the respective skill of the operators.'

That scientists are morally superior to any other human beings is debatable at least! Anyone who has carried out any active research knows that the kind of problems which crop up on a research team are very similar to the problems which repeatedly crop up in society at large. This fact was highlighted in James Watson's account of the discovery of the structure of DNA published under the title *The Double Helix*. In his foreword to Dr Watson's book, the late Sir Lawrence Bragg remarks in a masterful understatement '. . . one must admit that his intuitive understanding of human frailty often strikes home'.

Undoubtedly there have been some morally excellent scientists in every age. At the same time there have no doubt been just as many morally excellent milkmen. The main question is whether either of those sections of the community should have more power than the other in making the decisions. If the extra vote was to go to the man who had more contact in his everyday work with people and their problems, then there seems little doubt as to who should get it. Unfortunately, the scientist can only too easily stick to his laboratory in splendid isolation, only now and again peeping out through the test-tubes to see how the real world is getting on.

The history of intellectuals in general as moral arbiters of the nations is hardly an encouraging one. The fact that someone is educated and intelligent does not necessarily mean that he will be any the less evil for it, and nor that his cruelties will be any the less refined. Many of those who held senior positions in Himmler's SS in Nazi Germany were intellectuals, as described by Roger Manuell and Heinrich Fraenkl in their book *The Incomparable Crime*. And Richard Grunberger in the *Social History of the Third Reich* tells how 300 occupants of professional chairs addressed a manifesto to the electorate, asking them to vote for Hitler in March 1933. 'Many academics who were by no means committed Nazis welcomed the national wave as regenerative and healthy in essence, despite such regrettable side-effects as Jew-baiting and storm-troop brutality . . .' In Alistair Hamilton's *The Appeal of Fascism* there is a survey of the period 1919–45 in Italy, Germany, France and England. It gives a melancholy account of the support given to fascism by intellectuals, writers and artists.

When suggestions are made that groups of super-scientists in power might be the key to society's problems, somehow as a model it just does not seem to fit with the facts as we know them about man and his nature and limitations. We might perhaps be reminded rather of what Albert Einstein said when he realized the uses to which other scientists had put his theories. Einstein remarked that he wished he had become a blacksmith.

Some answers to the sources of man's problems which have been put forward in the name of science are really rather absurd. We mention them here to show the desperate attempts being made by people to try to get out of the hole into which science seems to have put them.

One of these suggested answers has all the characteristics of scientific mythology. It is rooted in the ideas of Dr Paul MacLean put forward in 1962. MacLean suggests that rather than possessing one single brain, man has basically three brains which coexist in each one of us. The oldest is basically reptilian, the second is genetically related to lower mammals such as the horse, and the third, says MacLean, represents the most recent phase of evolution which culminated in primates and gave man his superior mental characteristics. Man's behavioural problems are therefore caused by the animalistic tendencies of the more primitive brains which deal with functions such as sex, hunger, fear and aggression, and which conflict with our newly acquired powers of reason. As a result there is an antagonistic functional split in the form of a 'schizophysiology'.

These ideas have been taken up by Arthur Koestler in his book *The Ghost in the Machine*, published in 1968. Koestler writes: 'When one contemplates the streak of insanity running through human history, it appears highly probable that *homo sapiens* is a biological freak . . . the result of some remarkable mistake in the evolutionary process . . . Somewhere along the line of his ascent, something has gone wrong.' In the light of all this Koestler wants to turn 'maniac into man' by the discovery and distribution of a new drug which will have the effect of joining the various brains together, so reuniting reason and emotion. The 'hierarchic order' whereby emotion submits to reason will by this means be restored.

MacLean repeats his views in a recent collection of essays edited by Arthur Koestler and John Smythies called *Beyond Reductionism*. As Nigel Calder points out, this seems a curious place in which to put them, since no views could be more viciously reductionist in character.

In fact the chemistry of the brain is so complex that Koestler's simple mental stabilizer must forever remain a myth, quite apart from the doubtful validity of MacLean's ideas about split brains. There do indeed appear to be different centres of brain-control, but there seems little evidence that the processes of reason and emotion could possibly be separated so neatly. That this is so is a happy thought. What could be more dull, uninteresting and inhuman than a human being who showed no emotion?

If we are going to have to wait a long time for salvation by Koestler's magic drug, then it seems as if we are going to have to wait even longer for Dr Morris's biological solution. As he writes

E

in *The Naked Ape*: 'It takes millions of years to perfect a dramatically new animal model, and the pioneer forms are usually very odd mixtures indeed. The naked ape is such a mixture. His whole body, his way of life, was geared to a forest existence, and then suddenly . . . he was jettisoned into a world where he could survive only if he began to live like a brainy, weapon-toting wolf.' Waiting for all those genetic mutations which are going to adapt in a few 'millions of years' to our environment, like waiting for Koestler's pill to put in our drinking water, sounds a bit like waiting for Godot. One might perhaps be forgiven a touch of impatience at waiting a few hundred years, let alone a few million.

Answers of a rather more mundane kind are put forward by another biologist, Konrad Lorenz, at the end of his book *On Aggression*. In the final chapter entitled 'Avowal of Optimism', Lorenz grapples with the problem of how man is going to curb his natural aggressiveness, particularly as it has been vented in the destructive misuses of science. Four practical suggestions are given. First we must get to know ourselves better and try to find better directions into which we can channel our aggressive impulses – in sport for example. Second, there may be hope in sublimating our impulses with the help of a psychiatrist. Third, we must get to know people from other countries, and fourth there must be the 'intelligent and responsible channelling' of the 'militant enthusiasm of a younger generation'. So, says Lorenz, 'what is needed is the arousal of enthusiasm for causes which are commonly recognized as values of the highest order by all human beings, irrespective of their national, cultural or political allegiances.' But, even more than this, 'Sufficient knowledge of man and of his position in the universe would automatically determine the ideals for which we have to strive,' and Lorenz sees 'humour and knowledge' as 'the two great hopes of civilization'.

Now this is all very well, but as a model it hardly seems to stand up to the test of history. We have already had occasion to mention the enormous increase in knowledge over the past few hundred years, and there is no evidence to suggest that man has ever lacked a sense of humour. Furthermore, we are still left with a kind of moral vacuum in which there are no particular grounds why aggression should be channelled in one direction more than in another. According to Lorenz's biological system are there any *logical* reasons why aggression should be channelled into football rather than killing people? We are back to the old evolutionist fallacy that an 'ought' can somehow be extracted from an 'is'. Lorenz starts with the assumptions of an optimistically humanist position. But the validity of his assumptions is what the whole discussion is about, so it hardly clarifies the situation to start by assuming as axiomatic the very principles which are being called into question. And, to quote one reviewer, 'What happens to all those poor people who have neither knowledge nor a sense of humour?'

Humanists today are very well aware that their faith in reason and view of man as the measure of all things have not succeeded in generating any kind of value-system which is in any way essentially different from that of the Christian tradition out of which modern humanism sprang. As Professor Gwynne Jones puts it bluntly in a speech from which we have already had occasion to quote: 'I know no set of rationally derived ethical principles from which you can logically deduce rules to apply in real life, facing problems of moral choice.' This is an honest statement. 'Humanists,' says H. J. Blackham, 'do not dissent from the consensus of mankind down the ages on basic practical moral questions.' But today it is just these very basics which are under fire. It is significant that the humanism so popular in some British universities in the early 1960s very rapidly gave way to the much more anarchistic spirit of the later sixties. It is arguable that it was a logical progression.

Nor is there any lack of those who would like to give the so-called 'basics' a very thorough airing, as we saw in our discussion of society's current flight from reason and drift towards mysticism. In the process even the most basic 'basics' are being questioned, the very value and worth of man himself, which is a fundamental humanist assumption. Some years ago the writer

Norman Mailer was interviewed by David Leitch in *The Sunday Times*. Talking about murder Mailer said that 'I don't think anyone condemns murder *really*. Society may be founded on Kant's categorical imperative, but individual murder gives a sense of life to those around the event. Take newspaper readers – doesn't the suburban commuter get a moment of pleasure on the subway reading about murder? Is he perverse or is it really something life-giving? I prefer the second view of man, the less bleak one.'

One well-known humanist, Baroness Wootton, in a speech given to the Rationalist Press Association during 1971, said this: 'We urgently need a widespread educational programme for the development of an ethic which has no supernatural sanction. Rationalists believe that the only certain knowledge that we have about mankind is that human life begins at birth and ends at death. In the meantime we might as well make the best of it, and the way to do that is to evolve an appropriate ethic; not only for ourselves, but equally and even more for our neighbours. I think that the lack of this ethic may have something to do with disorderly trends which we find at present in our society . . .'

One cannot help feeling that the only reason that the British humanist tradition has kept going for so long is because we have been so protected from first-hand experience of humanism's more radical expressions, whether the Aryanism of Hitler's Nazi Germany, the cultured pessimism of French existentialism, or Marx's political humanism which now dominates more than a third of the world's population. Humanists would dissociate themselves from all three of these expressions, but the fact remains that for Hitler, Sartre and Marx there is one basic over-riding unifying factor – that man is the measure of all things. In the sheltered seclusion of a university common-room such troubling details seem very remote. For one who has choked at the acrid sting of tear-gas or stood with a group of stone-throwing Maoists behind a barricade being over-run by baton-wielding riot-police, the issues are only too real.

The humanist model does seem a very big pill to swallow. As

a representative of a late twentieth-century generation of under-
thirties, I am first asked to believe that I am the result of a purely
random evolutionary process. The only prerequisites for this
process are the presence of matter, time and chance. Because, by
some strange whim of fate, I and other men are the only physical
structures which happen to have been bestowed with a consciousness of their own existence, I am supposed to think of both
myself and others as being in some way more valuable than other
physical structures such as rabbits, trees or stones, even though in
a hundred years time the atoms of my decayed body may well be
indistinguishable from theirs. Furthermore the mass of vibrating
atoms in my head are supposed to have more ultimate meaning
than those in the head of the rabbit.

At the same time I am told that death is the end of the line. In
the time-scale of evolution my life is like a vapour which soon
vanishes. Whatever feelings of justice or injustice I may have in
this life, all my strivings, all my greatest decisions, will be
ultimately swallowed up in the on-going march of time. In a few
million years' time, a mere drop compared with the total history
of the earth, the memory of the greatest literature, the greatest
art, the greatest lives will be buried in the inexorable decay of the
Second Law of Thermodynamics. Hitler and Martin Luther King,
James Sewell and Francis of Assisi, Chairman Mao and Robert
Kennedy, all will be obliterated in the unthinking void.

So, I am told, I must make the best of a bad job. Even though I
have strong feelings of transcendence, a deep sense that I am more
than just a blind whim of evolution, I must nevertheless forget
such troubling questions, and concern myself with the real
problems of trying to live responsibly in society. Even though
my job involves studying man's brain as a machine, like any other
of nature's machines, I must still believe that man has some
special intrinsic worth which is greater than an animal's worth,
and while my emotions tell me that it may be true, I am not
given any more objective reasons for believing it.

At the same time I am given a broad set of ethics which I am
asked to practice. These are supposed to limit the extent to which

I am allowed to tread on my neighbour's toes. I must not tread on his toes any harder than I would like mine trod on. Unfortunately, when it comes to the crunch, I find that if there is something that I really want, then my nature is such that I am liable to tread on his toes anyway. Though slightly ashamed by this self-revelation, I am relieved to find that most other people discover that their natures tend to act in the same way.

Together with my self-revelation come some more puzzling observations and questions. I begin to see that international politics seem to reflect the basic failure of my nature rather faithfully, only of course on a much grander scale. Nations are all smiles and hand-shakes when things are going their way, but once they feel that their rights are being threatened in the smallest way, then the trouble begins. It all seems to add fuel to the initial suspicion that man's problem is not simply trying to find out what is good and evil, which is hard enough, but doing the good rather than the evil once he has found out. The dilemma is summed up beautifully by a picture on the front of the book *Objections to Humanism*, where someone with rather big feet is trying to pull himself up by his own boot-laces.

Furthermore, if all moral codes are relative, accepted as temporary conventions by society for the sake of its smooth running, then what happens when a society chooses to adopt values that are completely opposed to the original Christian world-view out of which modern humanism sprang? The humanist may well reject such new values out-of-hand. But on what logical grounds? Once a totalitarian state has control of the mass-media persuasion machinery, then it may indeed be able to mould public opinion into a whole new morality, where the value of the human individual becomes less than the value of the goals which the state is trying to achieve. The humanist might protest that Kant's categorical imperative says that human beings should never be treated as means to an end, but always as an end in themselves. But Kant's categorical imperative sprang from a Christian world-view. So, says the totalitarian state, we will strive for a new imperative in which the petty rights of the individual must be swallowed up in the greater purposes and goals of society as a whole. Once the new morality is generally accepted by society, by whatever means this acceptance may be brought about, then what possible logical objection could the humanist have to it?

We have by now landed feet first in Nazi Germany. Hitler, the mesmeric dictator, put in power by a majority vote, persuaded a large proportion of the population that one group of people were of intrinsically less value than another group. A new morality was agreed upon whereby the value of the individual became subordinated to the value of the Third Reich. Nazi doctors carried out horrible experiments on human subjects. Six million Jews were exterminated.

Today one third of the world's population is under the sway of a system where the 'new morality' stems from the basically humanistic assumption that man's unaided reason is the final arbiter of truth. 'Ours is a new morality,' wrote the Bolshevik *Red Sword* of 18 August 1919. 'Our humanism is absolute, for it has as its basis the desire for abolition of all oppression and tyranny. To us everything is permitted, for we are the first in the world to raise the sword not for the purpose of enslavement and oppression but in the name of liberty and emancipation from slavery. We do not wage war against individuals. We seek to destroy the bourgeoisie as a class.' In the struggle for power that followed the October revolution, *Pravda* revealed in its issue of 26 June 1921, that 'about 25 million people' were suffering from famine. Starvation took the lives of no less than five million people in Russia during 1921 and 1922.

In Lenin's interpretation of Marx's radical humanism people became digits in the expediencies of the struggle for power. Alexander Naglovsky writes in his *Reminiscences* of how Lenin once wrote a note to Dzerzhinsky, head of the Soviet secret police, asking him how many vicious counter-revolutionaries there were in prison at the time. Dzerzhinsky's reply was: 'About fifteen hundred.' Lenin read it, snorted something to himself, made a cross beside the figure, and returned the note to Dzerzhinsky.

The same night all fifteen hundred of the 'vicious counter-revolutionaries' were executed. The following day Lenin's secretary explained that there had been a mistake. Lenin usually put a cross on memoranda to indicate that he had read them and noted their contents. This little 'misunderstanding' cost fifteen hundred human beings their lives. Fifteen years later, in Stalin's great purges of the 1930s, millions more were exterminated for no better reason than that they had the wrong opinions.

We must remember that this tragic devaluation of the individual stems directly from Marxist theory. As Marx wrote in *The German Ideology*, 'The class . . . achieves an independent existence over and against individuals, so that the latter find their condition of existence predestined and hence have their position in life and their personal development assigned to them by their class, and become subsumed under it.' Yet as Professor Wright Mills has said, 'The ideals of a radical humanism in which man replaces God himself, accompanied by an Old Testament passion for human justice – these are among the mainsprings of Marx's career as a thinker . . .' So in the very act of becoming God it seems that man sows the seed of his own eventual devaluation and dissolution.

For over 700 million Chinese the 'new morality' has been clearly spelt out by Chairman Mao. 'In the political life of our country,' says Mao, 'how are our people to determine what is right and what is wrong in our words and actions?' Mao then goes on to outline six criteria whereby words and actions can be judged right or wrong. They are right if they:

'1. Help to unite the people of our various nationalities, and do not divide them;

2. Are beneficial, not harmful, to socialist transformation and socialist construction;

3. Help to consolidate, not undermine or weaken, the people's democratic dictatorship;

4. Help to consolidate, not undermine or weaken, democratic centralism;

5. Tend to strengthen, not to cast off or weaken, the leadership of the Communist Party;
6. Are beneficial, not harmful, to international socialist solidarity and the solidarity of the peace-loving peoples of the world.'

In other words what Mao says is right, what anyone else thinks is wrong. In the ferment of the Red Guard cultural revolution millions of people lost their lives because they held the wrong opinions.

The far-reaching implications of such radical humanist applications would of course be rejected by the vast majority of humanists in the West today. But if responsibility towards society is a basic humanist tenet, why can I not see my responsibility expressed in such political terms, especially when it may eventually lead to the extermination of so many evils in society? And if the majority of Chinese people accept Mao's ethics, as they seem to have done, then who can say them nay? If this is the kind of code that they want to choose to run society, then why shouldn't they? And if it be objected that they had no real choice, but the new code was forced upon them, so that it is not really an 'open society', then how can one tell the difference between the validity of a code which is apparently freely accepted, and one which is absorbed by the blanketing effect of the mass media?

If the completely relativistic attitude of the humanist towards morals raises plenty of nagging questions, then the findings of current scientific research that we outlined in chapter one raise even more. If ultimately man is just one more animal in the evolutionary tree, then why not make an animal-man chimaera? If man's value is only relative compared with other parts of nature, then why shouldn't we radically alter man's physical and mental structure by genetic engineering? If some kind of benefit could be found for society, then why shouldn't we produce clones of identical children? Now undoubtedly many of those kinds of manipulation would be unacceptable to most humanists, but it is difficult to see how this rejection could be rationally justified according to purely naturalistic principles. Again and again we are forced back to the same fundamental questions to which humanism has no answer. What is man? In the light of an apparently meaningless universe, does man have any real value? If so, why? Why should I be responsible to society when all my deeds will ultimately be obliterated in the sands of time? Why shouldn't I make personal pleasure my aim in complete disregard for everybody else?

The Christian values upon which science depends did not come from science itself. Now that the Christian basis has been removed, the thoughtful observer might be forgiven for wondering how long the traditional humanistic bias of the sciences can continue. Many might feel that C. S. Lewis's novel *Out of the Silent Planet* has more than a ring of truth when it depicts a humanist scientist who begins by making portentous claims for man, and ends by reducing man to a temporary manifestation of an all-pervading amoral and impersonal life-force.

Professor Jacques Monod has understood the situation very clearly. Monod has been likened to a kind of biochemical Albert Camus. His book *Le Hasard et la Nécessité* has been a best-seller in France, rivalling even De Gaulle's memoirs, and has now been published in English under the title *Chance and Necessity*. 'Man knows now,' says Monod, 'that he is like a gypsy camping on the edge of the universe where he must live. The universe is deaf to his music, indifferent to his hopes, as to his suffering or his crimes.' In a discussion on French television with a Communist and a Catholic, Monod berated Marx and Teilhard de Chardin alike for extracting purpose from history where he could only find necessity. Monod attacks Marx because he tries to explain the laws which govern nature by the laws which govern thought. And the laws that govern thought, according to the Marxist, are the Hegelian dialectical principles whereby one thought, the thesis, will be opposed by another thought, the antithesis, which will finally be resolved in a relativistic synthesis. But, says Monod, this is precisely what one does not find in nature. Nature proceeds by a long succession of errors, and the relation between DNA and proteins, for example, defies all dialectical description.

Monod is faithful up to a point to his own naturalistic assumptions. Nature simply happens, and that is all. There is no way of deriving an 'ought' from an 'is'. Modern societies have been robbed by science of any firm beliefs on which to base their value systems, and that, says Monod, is 'the greatest revolution ever to occur in our culture'. The universe is a chance universe – there is no necessity.

But now Monod makes a very big leap of faith. He says that although there are no logically derivable systems of ethics, nevertheless the pursuit of objective knowledge itself is an ethical activity, and there exist 'ethics of knowledge'. So the problem today is that 'society has accepted the fruits of science, but hasn't even heard of the ethics of knowledge upon which science is founded.' 'If society goes on living on science, while rejecting the moral code upon which it is based, that society is bound to collapse.' Similar ideas were expressed a long time ago by Dr J. Bronowski when he suggested that 'the deeper effect of science over the past three hundred years has been, not in the accumulation of true facts, but in making people aware that the very search for what is factually true is itself an ethical activity.' Dr Bronowski repeats these views in his book *The Identity of Man*.

Now unfortunately all this position does is bring us right back once again to what the discussion is all about. Science has only existed in so far as it has held onto the Christian view of reason, and the Christian values of the culture from which science stemmed. And it is equally true that society is collapsing as it attempts to throw out that moral code. But what Monod is trying to do is to support the code without its Christian basis. Yet if he is using strict objectivity to try to support objectivity as an ethical principle, then he has already put himself in the same cleft stick as the Vienna Circle with their Verification Principle. What objective reasons can Monod give for making objectivity an ethical principle any more than subjectivity? Along with a good proportion of modern artists we could indeed argue that the objectivity of 'man in the box' is the very thing that has reduced him to nothing.

Monod saves himself from thorough-going despair by the pragmatic adoption of an ethic which, according to his own assumptions, must by definition be self-annihilating. Other thinkers in the past have been much more willing to express the full weight of the despair that they feel in the midst of a seemingly random universe. Bertrand Russell, for example, reaches the limits of his pessimism in his *Free Man's Worship:* 'That Man is the product of causes which had no prevision of the end they were achieving; that his origin, his growth, his hopes and fears, his loves and his beliefs, are but the outcome of accidental collocations of atoms; that no fire, no heroism, no intensity of thought and feeling, can preserve an individual life beyond the grave; that all the labour of the ages, all the devotion, all the inspiration, all the noonday brightness of human genius, are destined to extinction in the vast death of the solar system, and that the whole temple of Man's achievement must inevitably be buried beneath the debris of a universe in ruins – all these things, if not quite beyond dispute, are yet so nearly certain, that no philosophy which rejects them can hope to stand. Only within the scaffolding of these truths, only on the firm foundation of unyielding despair, can the soul's habitation henceforth be safely built.'

Now let us put this model of the universe to the test. Does it fit with the kind of criteria suggested above? Clearly, with the assumptions of 'man in the box', the analysis of the situation is a very honest one. If this is man's real position, then let us face the consequences. But the fact of the matter is – our own humanness will not let us face the consequences. Being despairing all the time is rather boring. And we cannot in fact live like 'accidental collocations of atoms', because the conviction that our life seems to have some kind of meaning runs far too deep. This is seen extremely clearly in the life of Bertrand Russell himself, which was long and rich and thoroughly devoted to removing human injustices in a way which showed that he valued other human beings very highly. For that one can admire him. But what is not so clear is why Russell should have expected anyone else to share his views about the value of man when one considers the logical conclusions of his own world-view. There was a total split between his rational life and his real everyday life. They seemed to be in two water-tight compartments.

If one really accepts Russell's analysis of the universe given above which, after all, is only painting a clear picture of what it means to be 'man in the box', then the only truly reasonable conclusion would seem to be suicide. One student who committed suicide left behind this note: 'To anyone in the world who cares – Who am I? Why am I living? Where am I going? Life has become stupid and purposeless. . . The questions I had when I came to college are still unanswered and now I am convinced that there are no answers. There can only be pain, guilt and despair here in this world. My fear of death and the unknown is far less terrifying than the prospects of the unbearable frustration, futility and hopelessness of continued existence.'

So there is the tension. With the basic assumption that man is alone in the universe, man's reason tells him that he has no ultimate value. But he cannot live like that. He cannot put his view into practice. The only truly logical conclusion seems to be suicide, which at the same time seems the ultimate absurdity, the ultimate denial of his own humanity.

Those who believe that man is very firmly in the box are very aware of the problem. H. J. Blackham says that 'The most drastic objection to humanism is that it is too bad to be true. The world is one vast tomb if human lives are ephemeral and human life itself doomed to ultimate extinction.' But the replies which he attempts to give to his own objections seem so trivial when compared to the enormity of the issues involved. In his book *Humanism* Blackham writes that 'In any such reckoning, the ready money of daily cheerfulness and unalloyed pleasures is not too small to count.' One is reminded of the words of Aldous Huxley who is reported to have said a few minutes before dying on 22 November 1963: 'It is a little embarrassing to have been concerned all one's life by the human plight and yet having to realize at the end that all one has to offer as a warning is that one should "try to be a little more gentle".'

The problem for the humanist is to give answers which do not appear trite and trivial when measured alongside the profound problems and questionings of modern man at the end of the twentieth century. Somehow, when faced with moralistic injunctions to 'try a little harder', 'be more responsible', 'enjoy your daily pleasures', 'be more gentle', 'do your best', and so on, one might perhaps be forgiven for thinking that humanism is too bad to be true after all.

Fortunately there is a way which is at once more reasonable and more revolutionary.

Square one

We have already mentioned the way in which so many of our most basic assumptions are absorbed unconsciously and uncritically from our cultural environment. Indeed the very mass media themselves seem tailor-made to make this absorption as easy as possible. As Marshall McLuhan says in *Explorations in Communication*, 'All the new media, including the press, are art forms that have the power of imposing, like poetry, their own assumptions. The new media are not ways of relating us to the old "real" world: they *are* the real world, and they reshape what remains of the old world at will.'

We now soak up these basic assumptions almost from the moment at which awareness of our environment begins. America and Japan are perhaps the two countries where television has reached its most exalted position, though most other Western countries follow not far behind. It has been estimated that the average pre-school American child spends 64 per cent of his waking hours watching TV, and it has become commonplace to 'turn children over to the television set'. Dr Gerald Looney, of the University of Arizona, has calculated that by the time an American child reaches the age of 14, he will have seen 18,000 people die on television.

Some of the remarks made by the consumers in question during the course of this research are revealing. Amanda, aged four, told questioners: 'When a man gets shot on telly, the doctor takes off his skin and mends the hole in his tummy.' Another four-year-old, Andrew, added: 'People get into our television set through a little hole in the back. They're little picture people, and when they get shot and fall over and never wake up, it doesn't hurt them. Sometimes I laugh when they get killed.'

When reporters sent actual photographs of the Crimean War back to Britain, public opinion was shocked by the horrors that they presented. Today visual horrors have become part-and-parcel of the average television programme. Yet the impact is no longer there. Watching people die on a screen in the living-room seems to have the strange effect of whittling down the borders between fact and fantasy. Before the News there is a Western. Bang, bang, bang – people roll in the dust and are killed. Then there is the News. It is Vietnam or Northern Ireland – bang, bang, bang, people roll in the dust and are killed. In neither case is there any moral judgment. It just happens. Things are just there, that is all. In both cases there is the same sense of unreality. It is not so much the content of the mass media, but the assumptions behind the content, which have such a powerful effect on us.

One major assumption that is firmly embedded in most of what we absorb is the philosophy that assumes that man is in a closed-system universe. This presupposition is in the very cultural air that we breathe. So deep does it go, that if someone starts questioning or probing into this basic presupposition, then there is an uncomfortable feeling of being threatened, as if one of life's most treasured and traditional props was somehow going to be removed.

Yet we have seen that it is just this presupposition of 'man in the box' that seems to have landed man in such an extraordinary dilemma. If he uses his reason fully, then logically man himself seems to be dead and meaningless. If he wants to express the humanity that he most decidedly feels, then it seems only possible in mystical and anti-rational ways, and tied up in this flight from reason are the seeds of the death of science itself. And the whole dilemma stems from that basic first step of saying: 'In the beginning there was matter, time and chance, and that was all' – in other words, the basic presupposition which underlines the whole philosophy of rationalism. It just does not seem to be a model which fits either the facts about our reason or the facts about our humanity.

When we consider the mess that this presupposition has landed us in, it seems only honest and reasonable to question its validity. But of course presuppositions, by definition, cannot be 'proved' or 'disproved' in the same way that we could prove or disprove a mathematical formula. The very fact that they have to be assumed as starting-points emphasizes that their validity cannot be tested by such means. The only way they can be tested is by seeing whether the models that are built on them survive the tests of reason, time and human experience. If the models fail in this way, we are justified in questioning the assumptions which underlie them.

For instance I might accept as a basic presupposition from my childhood that all British people are inherently superior to any other race. For years I hold on to this conviction, and indeed build my whole view of international politics upon it. My interpretation of world news is filtered through this assumption. Then finally I venture forth across the Channel actually to test whether it is true. I soon meet some most delightful French people, and some charming Italians, and my world-view crumbles. My old presupposition is thoroughly shaken, so I go back to square one and adopt a new one: 'Every country is a mixed bag of individuals; some are nice and some are nasty.'

Now what happens when we go back and adopt the presupposition of the original scientists? The great majority of early scientists were theists. Their basic presupposition could be summed up in the words 'In the beginning God . . .' For them man was most definitely not in a box. The universe was open-ended; it was not a closed system. God not only existed, but the very existence and rationality of the universe stemmed from him.

As we discussed in chapter two, the Biblical theistic view of God sees every mechanism of the universe as depending directly on him; there are no gaps. He is continually active in the universe which he was, is and will be creating. Yet he is not the same as the universe, or nature. The early scientists were not pantheists.

In this Biblical view of God many picture-models are given to help us understand what he is like. He is seen first as being infinite. That is to say, he is not restricted by a space-time framework of reference. He is outside the limits of our familiar dimensions. Yet at the same time he is personal. When we talk about a person we mean someone who has a separate conscious identity from ourselves to whom we may assign certain characteristics. The person may be generous, or bad-tempered, or sensitive or artistic, and we assign these qualities according to the behaviour that we observe. The Biblical view of God is one which sees him as personal in this sense. He has a separate identity from us, and has certain characteristics in contrast to not having certain other characteristics. He is therefore both infinite and personal.

But, more than this, God himself is seen as a dynamic relationship of three persons. Between these three persons there is a perfect balance of unity and integrity. Each one is as much God as the other. This means that when we say God is love, we are not talking about some cold, static concept, but about a warm dynamic relationship which has always existed. This love has, is and will be expressed within the out-going action of the three persons in an eternal Trinity of dynamic self-giving. The same applies to the other characteristics of God, such as creativity, peace, perfection, gentleness and deep overwhelming joy. All these qualities have always existed in the universe in the same relationship. There has never been a void.

Many have jibbed at this idea of three-in-oneness because they have become side-tracked into thinking in mathematical rather than personal terms. But we are talking here about persons and not about mathematical symbols. In a human analogy we might think of Winston Churchill as being a statesman to the nation, the son of his mother and a friend of someone else. These are three roles of one single person expressed in three different ways depending on the context of the relationship. This analogy is not perfect but does express one aspect of a model which is trying to express what God is really like. It is as if we were in a flat world of two dimensions trying to understand the idea of a three-dimensional box. We could understand the idea of three separate two-dimensional squares, but the thought of there being three separate squares, which were at the same time just as much members of the same one box, would be beyond us. We are in the position of the physicist who is forced into the seeming paradox that light must be visualized both as particles and as waves at the same time, if he is to do justice to the physical data about light. The physicist today looks to fuller and more complete models to resolve this dilemma. Yet his model tells him a tremendous amount about light. In a similar way the idea of 'three in one' is a seeming paradox, yet as a model it is essential for doing justice to the data that we have on the Biblical concept of God, though in this case the dilemma will not be removed until we enter that 'extra dimension' itself.

There are a number of profound implications which stem from adopting the Biblical concept of God as our basic presupposition. Indeed there is not a single subject which we have yet discussed in this book which is not affected deeply by adopting this different starting point.

First there is the fact that science is possible. We have already seen how the methods of science flowed naturally from a Christian world-view. A God who is consistently upholding the universe makes rational science conceivable. The scientist is no longer faced with an unconscious step of faith before he can begin his science; instead his belief that experiments are reproducible stems directly from his belief in a rational God.

Second, man has a real and ultimate value. While the whole of creation is sustained by God, only man was made 'in God's image'. What does that mean? It means that only in man do we see a reflection of those characteristics which are rooted deeply in the nature of God himself. Man, like God, has a capacity for self-conscious thought, choice and self-awareness. Man, like God, is endowed with creativity and an appreciation of beauty. Man, like God, has the ability to love and be loved, to enter into relationships, and experience a deep overwhelming joy. In fact so close is the link between man and God, that man is even called a son of God. As made in the image of God he therefore has infinite value. This value is in no way relative; it is an absolute value which depends on an absolute God. A person's worth therefore depends not on his colour, political views, place in society, IQ, education, success, income-bracket, state of health, popularity or how useful he is as a means to any particular end, but on the fact that God has given him infinite value which is intrinsic in the very fact that he is a human being. This assumption therefore gives a far more exalted view of man than the humanistic presupposition of man in the box, where, as we have seen, an inexorable logic finally reduces him to nothingness.

Third, the creator-relationship between God and the universe means that there is meaning as well as mechanism. The universe is going somewhere. There is a purpose. The experience of loving therefore becomes not a hollow laugh in an empty universe, but a human reflection of something which has always been there. The feeling of awe and worship is no longer the mindless freak of a chance process of evolution, but a natural response to the one who made us (by whatever process it might have been carried out). Moments of exultant joy cease to be random lights in another wise grey world, but rather like paintings of that deep joy which has always existed within the dynamic personality of God's three-in-oneness. Feelings of deep humanness therefore stem from the personality of God himself. My very ability to communicate and express feelings in words comes from a personal God who speaks and shares.

A direct consequence of our shift in presupposition has been that we can now use our heads with impunity. It is the logic of this position that the breach between man's reason and humanness is healed. On this assumption the more we use our reason, the more human does man seem to become, and the more significant his existence in the universe. All our feelings of humanity, all our feelings of purpose, direction and importance 'fit' with a state of affairs that is actually happening, that is really taking place. They are not illusions.

Our reason is therefore released from the dead-ends of a naturalistic position. No intellectual schizophrenia is necessary, because the world of reason and the world of feeling belong to the same one God who is the source of both. Each makes sense of the other. The atoms bouncing around in my brain therefore become the mechanistic correlates of a mind which faintly reflects the mind of God himself. The linguistic concepts embodied in my consciousness find their ultimate source in the personal God who speaks. At the same time the more subjective and emotional side of my life finds its roots in a God who feels. There is one God for one whole human being. There is no 'schizo-physiology'.

All we are doing here is exploring some of the immediate consequences which flow from presupposing that the Biblical view of God is correct. It should be emphasized that we are not attempting to 'prove' the existence of God in any kind of rigorously philosophical or even mathematical way. If such a proof were possible, then we would certainly not end up with the God of Christianity. Instead we would end up with some philosophical concept that would be no greater than the system we had thought up, and the logical conclusion would be to worship the person who thought up the system rather than the idea that had apparently been proved. The Biblical God is not a dry abstract idea waiting to be slotted into some neat system. He is the dynamic, acting source of all life, thought and purpose, or he is not God at all. Trying to prove his existence would be rather like a river trying to prove that it arose in a spring, or an actor in a play trying to show mathematically that the author of the play existed.

Indeed, if we are attempting to use the word 'prove' in any mathematical or philosophical sense, then it is a well-known fact that I cannot even 'prove' my own existence, nor that of somebody else. It is rather a deeply embedded presupposition which is summed up in all that we mean when we use that little word 'I'. In fact what we are concerned with here is the use of the word 'proof' in a much more general open-ended scientific way, in which it refers to our belief that we find a certain model very persuasive because it appears to fit so many facts. So when, for example, we accept as a model of explanation that the Christian God exists, the persuasiveness of the model lies in what happens when we start tracing the logical results of this acceptance, and not in some kind of systematic mathematical or philosophical 'proof'.

There are certainly no strictly scientific data which could possibly have any bearing on the existence or non-existence of God. The scientist, as a scientist, is neutral. As we saw in chapter two, mechanism and meaning are two complementary ways of looking at the same thing. They are not contradictory. When a scientist makes measurements and gathers data from a mechanistic universe, there is no way in which, acting purely according to the methodology of science, he could deduce whether there was any meaning in the mechanism or not.

In fact there is no evidence that being a scientist leads people not to believe in God. Indeed the opposite is often true. Sometimes it is just those who are most aware of mechanism at a scientific level who are made aware of the need for meaning at another level. As Professor Robert Boyd, Professor of Physics at London University, said in a recent interview: 'I think it is quite as common to find Christians among scientists as in any other profession. In fact, I would say that, if anything, it is a little commoner to find Christians among physicists than it is in some other branches of science.'

There have been a number of recent surveys carried out on the beliefs of university students. Two extensive surveys carried out by different investigators at the University of Harvard and the University of Ghana tested the following hypothesis, that:

a General university education leads to a decline in supernatural belief; and
b Scientific training in particular hastens this decline.

Neither of these hypotheses were supported by the data obtained. Other similar surveys have come to the same conclusions.

One of the most startling suggestions made by some theologians is to maintain that our current ways of thinking about God should be changed. Apparently to think of God as Father is out of date in our scientific age. The idea that he is 'up there' or 'out there', or in any way separate from our existence, is to use spatial language which, we are told, is not justified because we no longer believe in a three-decker universe of heaven above, earth in the middle, and hell underneath. In the place of these so-called 'out-dated' ideas about God, we are asked to accept various concepts similar to those which appeared in the Hindu writings called the *Upanishads*, a collection of 'teachings for a disciple' which appeared in India around the sixth century BC. According to these teachings God is seen as the 'Ultimate Reality', the 'Deepest Self' or the 'Ground of All Being'. Similar ideas have been revived at various other periods, for example by Spinoza in the seventeenth century, and then finally by various theologians in Western countries during the past thirty years, the most publicized example being Dr John Robinson.

What is so puzzling is the idea that it is somehow more 'scientific' to express ideas about God in these seemingly non-spatial terms. The very essence of a model is that it communicates something which is not the thing itself, but a representation of the thing. We have already seen how scientists commonly use models and pictures of reality to carry on their work. But no biochemist really thinks that the double-helical model of DNA, that looks so comfortingly persuasive when built out of plastic balls and little sticks in the laboratory, is really what he would see if a DNA molecule could be blown up in size so that he could look at it. Similarly no physicist really expects that if only he had a slightly different kind of eye-sight, he would be able to see light travelling along as literal waves in space. In each case the model provides a useful representation of certain data. But the model is not the thing itself.

It has been pointed out by a number of philosophers that words themselves are rather like models. When I say the word 'rain', then immediately a three-dimensional internal model flashes into my brain which represents the idea of wetness and little drops of water coming down from above. The word itself is not wet, and neither is the representation which flashes into my brain. It would be ridiculous to mistake the word for the rain itself. Rather it acts as a model to communicate immediately certain important internal images. Indeed a number of research teams are at present trying to find out how these internal spatial images are represented in the brain itself.

Now, as we have noted, the Bible builds up our idea of God by a wide range of complementary word-pictures, each of which gives us one aspect of the nature of God. Clearly, to communicate the idea of an infinite God to a finite mind, a very large number of models are needed, and some of these in our finite space-time world may naturally seem paradoxical. Equally clearly, the communication about God could never be exhaustive. A finite mind could never obtain a full grasp and understanding of an infinite being without itself being infinite.

So when David in the Psalms says that the 'Lord is my shepherd', he is saying something very profound. He is saying that God cares for him in the same way that a shepherd looks after his sheep. The model 'shepherd' is something which immediately communicates certain essential activities of God. David did not really think that God had a crook and was wandering about heaven looking for good grazing spots. He did not make the mistake of confusing the model with the person that it was partially representing.

It is an interesting fact that some people tend to think in very visual ways, and others in a much more abstract way. For instance some memorize the content of a page by visualizing the actual page and the position of the words on it, whereas others memorize by the intrinsic logic of what they are trying to remember. Professor Grey Walter has shown, by measuring the brain-waves of various classes of people who think either visually or more non-visually, that there seems to be a distinct difference in certain waves between the two types of people. The slightly different ways of conceptualizing seem to depend on small differences in brain-structure. From this fact stems the celebrated remark of Lenin that 'I have yet to meet a single woman who can do these three things: Understand Marx, play chess or read a railway timetable.'

So someone who thinks of God as Father in very visual terms should not be criticized for being 'out of date', any more than should someone who thinks of the model in a very abstract way. The important point is whether the content of the model is true, not the exact way in which the model is held in the brain.

The structure of our brains themselves is three-dimensional, and our sensory input suggests a spatial universe. So it is hardly surprising that we think spatially. To suggest that 'man come of age' should therefore think non-spatially is absurd. Our very language is thoroughly permeated with spatial concepts which communicate certain essential facts. For instance I may be 'top' of the class, or 'bottom' of the class. At work I am 'promoted' or 'demoted'. A man goes 'up' in the world or 'down' in the world. The sun 'rises' and the sun 'sets'. A president of a country is at the 'head', not the 'feet'. So when we say that God is 'head over' all the universe, we are not referring to his presence at a particular point in space, but to the fact that he is ultimately the One through whom the universe exists. In the same way, when we say that heaven is 'up' we are describing its 'higher' quality of life as compared to life on earth, not talking about its position in space.

So when certain theologians suggest that we consider the Christian God as the 'ground of our being', there are several immediate objections. First, the statement is essentially mystical. It seems to have no possible content which could be analysed or talked about. Rather it reflects the current drift towards mystical ways of thinking which are basically anti-rational. We can understand the four words used in the phrase, but when put together they communicate nothing, except perhaps to the person who uses them to try to express a certain feeling that he is experiencing. The phrase therefore comes in the same category of statements as those used by someone on a drug trip. For example certain vivid experiences might lead a person high on LSD to say that 'Ultimate reality is blue with pink spots'. This might be an attempt to express a very intense experience, but it would not communicate anything. The essence of mystical experience is that rational communication is dead.

Secondly if the phrase 'ground of our being' is an attempt to express the Christian concept of God in new terms, then it hardly seems to have met with the required results. One has the utmost sympathy with the small boy who, on being told that God was the 'ground of his being', asked whether God was rather like the contents of the digestive tract of earthworms which he was fond of cutting up in the garden! As a model it hardly seems the best one for communication. Furthermore it seems to be suggesting the rather pantheistic idea that God is part of each of us, in contrast to the Christian theistic view that there is a God who is there, personally distinct from us, though upholding the whole universe by his continuing creativity. It does seem therefore as if the theologians, in a no doubt honest attempt to express themselves more clearly, have paradoxically tried to describe God by taking away the very type of spatial model with which scientists are most familiar.

As Professor Malcolm Jeeves, Professor of Psychology at the University of St Andrews, has written in *The Scientific Enterprise and Christian Faith*, expressing the view of thirty-six Christian scientists who took part in an international conference at Oxford: 'In seeking to express the activity of God in this world and in our own lives in terms which we can understand, we must use models taken from this world, we must make use of images, pictures, parables and stories from the everyday happenings in this world, otherwise it seems that we must say nothing at all. As scientists we have learned how necessary our models, analogies, images and pictures are in assisting our understanding of physical reality and of communicating this understanding to each other. Perhaps we may be forgiven for reminding the theologians that all the time we are making such extensive use of concepts like electrons, waves, genes, species, reflex arcs, nerve nets and so on, without which we should be completely lost both in our understanding and in our communication with each other, we are nevertheless careful not to identify the models with the reality they represent.'

We have seen therefore that in adopting the Biblical concept of God as our starting presupposition, we have not been involved in any thought-processes which are different from those of our familiar everyday world of people and things. At the same time we have seen some of the fundamental implications about man and the universe which stem from this presupposition. But it might be objected at this point that this God is of our own creation, someone brought in to solve otherwise insoluble problems, a convenient philosophical postulate to give the universe some meaning. Are we not just trying to escape from the terrible dilemma of 'man in the box' by a piece of wishful thinking?

Clearly this would be the case if we were just speculating about what we thought God was like. He would simply be the God of our own making and choosing, rather on the lines of the title of a recent book called *The God I Want*. Any such speculations must be doomed to failure. How could a finite mind, simply by its own processes of reasoning, possibly find out what an infinite God was really like? If God has not communicated to us, then surely there is nothing else to say? We would, by definition, be confined to silence about the whole subject.

This is why we have consistently used the phrase 'the Biblical concept of God'. This is rooted in the conviction that in the Biblical record God has in fact spoken through nations, individuals and historical situations. If we allow the assumption that there is a personal God, then it is natural to believe that he is a God who communicates, a God who speaks. It is the Biblical claim that God *has* spoken.

This is where the use of the word model in this religious sense differs from its use in a scientific context. The scientific model is something which we invent, and which is a temporary way of fitting together certain data. Eventually it will be replaced by a better model. The model of God with which we are presented in the Bible is not something we invent, but something 'given'. In other words it is painting for us a view of God which we could never have known just by sitting down and thinking about it.

There is nothing at all unreasonable about God speaking and revealing himself in this way. Indeed there is much evidence to suggest that it is only as man is willing to acknowledge this self-revelation that his own nature, rationality and world-view will begin to make some kind of sense. But even as we say this, other questions are being raised. What is the character of this revelation? Is it convincing enough to persuade us that man is not in a closed-system universe after all? And, even more than this, can God be known?

To answer some of these questions we must turn to consider the culmination of that revelation himself.

The true radical

There are some big problems which have to be overcome by anyone in our post-Christian culture who seriously tries to consider the life and work of Jesus Christ. One problem is that strange assortment of misconceptions which often filters down to us from childhood days. Jesus, along with Father Christmas and Davey Crockett, is somehow reserved to that corner of our minds dealing with childhood memories, where the borders between fact, fantasy and dream have become eroded. Often the picture of Jesus Christ that finally emerges is of a slightly anaemic long-haired figure who wanders across the pages of a childhood Bible or catechism, possibly trailed by a few rather miserable-looking sheep. The idea left behind is one of ineffectuality and irrelevance to real life.

Our first task, therefore, is to be willing to part with this obsolete crust of dim memories, and be ready to face up to the real Jesus Christ. This means that we must be willing to jettison second-hand ideas, and go back to the original documents themselves. It is extraordinary how many people make sweeping statements about the life of Christ, when a little research reveals that they have never in fact during their entire adult life even read through the New Testament.

The documents of the New Testament are historically extremely well accredited, as has been shown in the book *The New Testament Documents* by Professor F. F. Bruce. During the past fifty years many valuable documents have been discovered which have extended considerably the trustworthiness of the historical data, until today we have no less than 5,000 Greek manuscripts of the New Testament in whole or in part. Some of these documents were being widely circulated very shortly after they were written. At the same time considerable archaeological data have been collected which support in detail the historical and geographical facts mentioned in the New Testament. In Luke's Gospel the names of officials, positions of state boundaries, and even the detailed positions of small villages have been confirmed by external evidence. Such has been the persuasiveness of the archaeological evidence collected during the past fifty years, that many leading scholars have shifted their position with regard to the Biblical text from a cautious scepticism to a thorough-going affirmation of its reliability.

A detailed survey of the historicity of the New Testament is outside the scope of this book. But it is important because it emphasizes that the world of the New Testament is a real world. It is not a dream world, or a mythical world, or a mystical world. It is the world of historical people, of Mary, Peter, Paul and Pontius Pilate. It is a world of rough fishermen, fussy bureau-cratic tax-men and smooth rich officials. It is a world dominated by politics, by the presence of a totalitarian state, by the constant threat of armed revolution. Things in this world are as real as things in our own world. It is not like the world of Greek legends, or transcendental meditation, or the psychedelic colours of an LSD trip. Tables and coloured cloth and bowls and fish, the wood of the cross itself, had the same sight, feel and smell as they do today.

So Jesus comes to us as a very real person. He is very human.

He likes people. He constantly mixes with them; he is constantly involved with them. Most of his life is spent banging away as a carpenter making tables and chairs. He is really upset when a close friend dies. He gets hungry. He knows the games of the local kids.

At the same time Jesus chose not to conform to the social pattern of his day. He was not interested in maintaining the status quo or keeping up with the Joneses. He was sickened by the slick, trite professionalism of the religious leaders of the day. He used to call them 'blind guides', 'hypocrites', 'white-washed tombs', 'brood of vipers'. He preferred to mix with those whom society regarded as cast-offs, such as crippled people, thieves, prostitutes, and the hated tax-collectors. Somehow, for him, the value of human beings seemed to lie just in the fact that they were human.

As we start reading through the life of Christ afresh, we find one who was passionately committed to a life-long revolution – but a revolution of love in which he died to his own feelings and needs for the sake of others. The focus of his attention was constantly on others, others, others. His world was clearly not a closed-system universe. God was most definitely in action. Miracles really happened.

A truly scientific attitude at this point can be a great help. This is the attitude which approaches evidence with no particular preconceived notions. It is willing to follow the evidence wherever it might lead, providing that it is convincing enough. Unfortunately many approach the New Testament with a mind already completely soaked in the basic presupposition of Rationalism, that the universe is a closed system. But it is more rational and reasonable in fact to adopt the more open-minded position, which is at least willing to admit that something out of the ordinary could take place, and the question is whether there is enough historical evidence for it.

The miracles of the New Testament are clearly supernatural in character, though of course we could find natural explanations for a small proportion of them in psychosomatic medicine. But when it comes to a dead man called Lazarus who had been dead for four days, and whose body was smelling because it had started to decay, whom Jesus then raised from the dead so that the normal processes of body decay were reversed, we are clearly somewhat out of the range of psychosomatic medicine. A claim is being made here that something supernatural has taken place – that is, something which does not naturally or normally take place.

Now when we use the word 'supernatural', it does not mean that what we call supernatural is any more or less an activity of God than any other aspect of nature. The whole of nature is a continual expression of God's active creativity, the natural as much as the supernatural. In that sense the tree growing outside the window is as much a miracle as the raising of Lazarus; they are both activities of God. Yet the word 'miracle' is still useful because it describes an unusual working of God in contrast to the usual. I would clearly be more surprised by the raising of Lazarus than I would be by the growth of the tree. It is the unusualness of the event which makes me call it supernatural.

Once I accept that we are living in a closed-system universe, then by definition miracles could not happen, or at any rate there would be no reason to expect them to happen. This is why David Hume's arguments against miracles ultimately turn out to be long strings of tautologies. Once Hume accepted that there was nothing outside a closed system universe, then clearly he would have to be extremely sceptical about any miraculous claims. Considering his presupposition, Hume would have been illogical to suggest otherwise. So when he wrote that 'A miracle is a violation of the laws of nature; and as a firm and unalterable experience has established these laws, the proof against a miracle from the very nature of the fact, is as entire as any argument from experience can possibly be imagined', the same point applies. If there is just matter and energy in the universe, and it appears to behave in a reproducible way, then there would be no particular reason for believing that it would act in a non-reproducible way. Hume would have been very silly had he concluded differently.

One's attitude to miracles depends completely therefore on one's basic presupposition. Immediately one has adopted the presupposition of 'man in the box' then any further arguments against miracles would have to be tautologies, mere repetitions of the basic assumption, only using different words. A closed-system universe must lead automatically to a closed mind on such issues.

For the theistic scientist, however, the situation is very different. His work in his research is but to 'think God's thoughts after him'. If one of God's thoughts expressed in nature is slightly different from the way his thoughts are normally expressed, then that is natural in light of the fact that it is God himself who is sustaining the whole of nature anyway. Furthermore, it is the context of the thought which is important, not simply the abstract fact that it happened. The raising of Lazarus was a vivid illustration of the fact that Jesus had power over the grave, and was carried out in the context of his teaching on the subject. When he healed people, it was to express his compassion and love. It was the meaning of the miracle, not just the fact that it took place, that was significant.

The scientist, using simply the methods of scientific research, must be strictly an agnostic when it comes to the question of miracles, just as he must over the question of the existence of God. There is nothing in his methodology which could possibly be brought to bear on the question. For him it is a historical question and not a scientific question. It has been the mistake of certain theologians, who have held the almost mystically rigid causality view of science so common in the last century, to claim, like Hume, that in the light of the so-called 'laws of science', miracles must therefore be excluded. We have already seen how this naively deterministic view of science has been discarded during this century. Yet they have insisted on wading through the New Testament, with their nineteenth-century scientific assumptions, in an attempt to 'demythologize' its content – in other words to discard anything that seems slightly miraculous. The result is rather what one would expect: a dry skeleton of a man's life with all the really essential parts missed out.

No, the real Jesus who walked and taught in first-century Israel did things which were unashamedly supernatural. Provided that

we do not approach him with some presupposition which automatically closes our minds, then we can be ready to make an
honest assessment of the evidence for his miracles. For there is
plenty of it, and not only from the obvious historical documents
which make up the New Testament. For instance, the fact that
Jews in the first century were forced to accuse Jesus of practising
magic is good evidence from his most sceptical opponents that
he had in fact been performing something quite out of the
ordinary. Rabbi Eliezer Hyrcanus spoke in AD 95 of 'Jesus' magic
art'. A formula of damnation which runs 'Jesus practised magic
and led and seduced Israel' was recorded in Jewish writings at
about the turn of the century, and may have originated in the
Great Sanhedrin of AD 32.

Having cleared our minds of some mental blocks that might
otherwise have prevented us listening to what Jesus really had to
say, we can now turn our attention to two main strands of Jesus'
teaching which are of the utmost significance for many issues that
have been raised in previous chapters. The first is the radical
assessment that Jesus made of man himself, and the second is the
realistic appraisal that he made of human society. Once again, if
we are to assess Jesus' solutions to man's dilemmas with an
open mind, then we must be continually asking the basic question:
as models of explanation, do they fit the facts as we know them?

At the heart of Jesus' teaching was the fact that he saw man as
being truly responsible for his actions, that he was not like some
programmed machine that has no real choice. And because man
is truly responsible, it is reasonable that he should bear the
consequences of this responsibility. For example Jesus once said
that 'On the judgment day everyone will have to give account of
every useless word he has ever spoken. For your words will be
used to judge you, either to declare you innocent or to declare
you guilty.' In other words, what we say is not just swallowed
up in the on-going march of time, but it has a real significance
in the light of eternity. Jesus gives an enormous value to man
himself: we are not like a piece of kinetic art whose essence lies
in its very transience, but more like a Rembrandt where the

'message' in the painting goes far deeper than simply the people and objects represented on the canvas.

The fact that man is truly responsible for his actions is something that we emphasized in chapter two. Anyone looking at man, however mechanistic their description of him may be, must be forced to the conclusion that he has a real freedom of choice – that there is no prediction which could be made about his decisions which could be binding upon him whether he liked it or not. This ability to choose is essential to Jesus' teaching. Without it there would of course be no basis for responsibility or punishment.

The tendency in recent years has been to treat criminal offenders as patients rather than as breakers of the law. Punishment is therefore seen as primarily remedial. Strangely enough this shift in emphasis has been made in the name of humanity. Yet there can be nothing more degrading to a man than treating him as mentally sick rather than as a morally responsible free agent. One characteristic of sickness is that it may well be incurable. Once someone is punished for a wrong action, whether at the level of childhood misbehaviour, or at the level of a crime against society, then there can be a real freedom from guilt after the punishment is over. But immediately we say that someone commits a crime because they are 'sick', then we may be condemning them to a lifetime of guilt over the fact that they have this 'sickness' in the first place.

Clearly there is a small class of criminals who are suffering from extensive brain damage or severe mental retardation who have reduced responsibility. Also it has been put forward at various times that certain genetic anomalies may lead to an increased chance of crime, though often such suggestions have had to be withdrawn in the light of further research. For example in 1965–6 it was widely held that an extra Y chromosome was more common amongst the criminal population than the general population, and the idea received much publicity with the news-paper idea of a 'criminal gene'. However the evidence for the theory has now dwindled almost to nothing, and in a careful survey of the literature carried out by Dr Griffiths, Medical

F

Officer at Wandsworth Prison, he concludes that 'it is probable that the large majority of XYY subjects are not in prisons or psychiatric hospitals' and that 'the characteristics of those with XYY chromosomes are not very different from controls also taken from a prison population.' Even if certain genetic abnormalities are found in higher proportions amongst prison populations, the difficult but crucial question has still to be asked: 'Was their wrong decision binding on them whether they liked it or not?'

What is quite clear is that there is no evidence to contradict the insistence of Jesus that people have true moral responsibility for their actions, though in the small number of cases where there is extensive reduction of that responsibility, ultimately it is only God himself who could really judge the extent of the reduction, or whether it had even ceased to exist altogether. In no sense therefore does Jesus treat people as programmed machines who have no real choice about what they are going to do with their lives. At the same time Jesus was well aware that the way evil is expressed depends considerably upon the environment. It is not the environment which produces the evil, but at the same time the environment may strongly influence the particular manner and direction in which that evil is channelled. The contrast between various ways that Jesus dealt with different members of society is very striking. His approach towards those whose environment had led them into more dramatic crimes against society showed extreme sensitivity and gentleness, especially when such people showed some awareness of their need. However, only a withering scorn was reserved for the smug pride of the Pharisees which he so heartily repudiated. For Jesus the essence of evil lay in that attitude which is unwilling to admit that it needs help.

If Jesus had an extremely high view of the responsibility of man, then his assessment of man's real problems was radical in the deepest sense of that word. In surveying earlier on in this chapter some of the answers currently being served up to solve man's dilemmas, it was noticeable that one common theme ran through all of them. In each case the blame for responsibility, and the source of the cure, was placed outside man himself. In the humanist type of answer, what was needed was a better environment, better education, more social services and so on. In the more biological answers, then the cause of our problem seemed to be that we had not evolved enough, or by evolving in the wrong way we had ended up with a split brain which was 'really' the cause of all our problems. Some of the political answers suggested handing over more power to groups of scientists who could more ably control the results of their experiments. Whatever the answers, it seemed that man's basic problems were something 'happening' to him, rather than being caused by him.

Now Jesus stated most definitely that there was something basically wrong with man himself. He was saying that evil was not a slight temporary problem which would soon become ironed out by an improved environment, but something rooted in the nature of man himself, and which only a major internal revolution could destroy. So when Jesus was commenting on the Jewish leaders' habits of going through long ceremonial washings, he said that 'It is what comes out of a person that makes him unclean. For from the inside, from a man's heart, come the evil ideas which lead him to do immoral things, to rob, kill, commit adultery, covet, and do all those sorts of evil things; deceit, indecency, jealousy, slander, pride, and folly – all these evil things come from inside a man and make him unclean.' The word 'heart' referred to what we would now sum up by the words conscience, mind and will. It had very little connotation of emotion, which is what we connect with the word today. Therefore Jesus is saying that in our innermost being we are morally warped. His picture of man is reflected in modern psychoanalysis where the subconscious is seen rather like a stagnant pool; when we push a stick down and give a good stir, then a lot of rather nasty things come up to the surface.

The whole of the New Testament is uniformly consistent in seeing something as being wrong in man himself. As Jesus said in another context: 'The light has come into the world, and men loved darkness rather than light, because their deeds were evil.'

James, in his letter, remarks that the basis for wars and fighting comes from the very nature of man: 'Where do all the fights and quarrels among you come from? They come from your passions, which are constantly fighting within your bodies. You want things, but you cannot have them, so you are ready to kill; you covet things, but you cannot get them, so you quarrel and fight.' It should be emphasized that all these analyses of man are based on man's responsibility for his evil actions; they are not saying that it is simply his emotions which have gone astray. It is man's will which is the central problem.

Now this is neither a pessimistic nor an optimistic view of man, but a realistic view. It is facing up to the facts of human nature as they really are, and not as we would like them to be. Clearly this analysis of man fits with the evidence that we surveyed when considering various extrapolations made from biological evolution. Man always seems to have had the same basic nature in every age. Evil has always been rampant. It has never been eradicated by improved education, or a higher standard of living, or scientific advances. Hilaire Belloc's couplet somehow sticks in the throat when spoken in the 1970s:

> 'When science has discovered something more,
> We shall be happier than we were before.'

Swinburne's ecstatic utterance, 'Glory to man in the highest, for man is the master of things', might equally make us shudder. The statement of at least one 'honest materialist', Dr Henry Miller, seems much more realistic: 'Science and technology have equipped man to control most of his biological competitors, from wolves to viruses. Today he himself is his only real enemy . . .'

Even after the most traumatic political revolutions the same problems immediately crop up again with monotonous regularity, simply because the nature of man himself remains the same. After the French Revolution millions felt a deep sense of betrayal of the very principles of the revolution as Napoleon exerted his dictatorship. Trotsky in *The Revolution Betrayed* and, more passionately, Daniel Cohn-Bendit in *Obsolete Communism*, describe how the Russian revolution drifted inevitably into a bureaucratic dictatorship with all the old problems that society faced before the revolution. As Trotsky writes, remarking on the period in the early twenties immediately after the civil war: 'The demobilization of the Red Army of five million played no small role in the formation of the bureaucracy. The victorious commanders assumed leading posts in the local soviets, in economy, in education . . . Thus on all sides the masses were pushed away gradually from actual participation in the leadership of the country.' 'We are not Utopians,' Lenin proclaimed in his book *State and Revolution*, 'We want the Socialist Revolution with human nature as it is now. Human nature itself cannot do without subordination . . . There must be submission to the "armed vanguard" . . . until the people will grow accustomed to observing the elementary conditions of social existence without force and with subjection.' It would perhaps be unkind to remark that the process of 'growing accustomed' seems to be going on for an inordinately long time . . .

Every man, in his quieter moments of self-reflection, has to face up to the fact that he is basically selfish. This selfishness is not just a biological mechanism of self-preservation, but goes far beyond the basic needs of survival. Of course we will go through the most incredible contortions to try to evade the point. But it is a fact that our most altruistic actions can be tinged with a smug self-righteousness, that rather self-satisfied feeling that we are 'doing the right thing'. Even when we measure ourselves according to our own personal codes of conduct, however limited these might be, we are still left with the uncomfortable feeling that we have somehow missed the mark. Of course Jesus went much further. He not only hammered home the validity of the law of Moses, but went beyond it in tackling the question of basic motivation. Jesus said that anger was as bad as murder, that we could not take revenge, that we should not just love our friends but our enemies as well. He even said that we should love other people in the same kind of practical ways that we love and look after ourselves. As we read through the Sermon on the Mount it all seems so impossible. We are condemned. No one could actually live like that by their own efforts. It is like a plumb-line that shows up our smallest distortion and imperfection. Our natural reaction is to run, to escape. It's our genes, our environment, our extrovert personality or our introvert personality. It's the weather, the political system, the people next door, the 'evils of society', the hang-over from last night, the yapping of the dog . . . Anything to avoid personal responsibility for that explosion of temper, that burst of irritability, that biting comment that hurt someone else, that vicious piece of driving, that deliberate building-up of our image, that fiddling of the tax forms, that determination to stand on our rights and hang everyone else. The very fact that all these things are accepted as 'natural' is perhaps an indication that we need to take a long cool look at the kind of model of humanity that Jesus was talking about. Somehow our model of the 'normal human being' seems a rather warped and distorted idea when we measure it up against the life and personality of Jesus Christ.

Some, of course, will close their eyes to such uncomfortable questions. Selfishness becomes so embedded that we cease to recognize it for what it is. We placidly assume that the 'evils of society' are things which have nothing to do with us. We erect little materialistic cotton-wool barriers round our lives to ward off nagging questions. We retreat behind clichés like 'I've never done anyone any harm' or 'I'm no worse than anyone else' or 'I always give people a helping hand', and we think that in this we have somehow found our true humanity. Yet all this can just be escapism, an attempt to run away from what we are really like. Our lives are like dusty window-panes. In the semi-gloom of our own moral barrenness we think the glass is clean. It is only as we allow them to be exposed to the light of Jesus of Nazareth that we realize what a murky picture of humanity our lives in fact represent.

For Jesus, a realistic assessment of human society in general flowed directly from his radical analysis of human nature. He held out no glib utopian hopes for this world. He saw the problems of society as being rooted in the selfishness of man. The problems of humanity are like large-scale paintings of the problems of each individual. Personal greed leads to national greed. Personal jealousy leads to national jealousy. The individual family is like a microcosm of a macroscopic society where all the tensions, trials, quarrels and fears of family life are reproduced on a large scale in the lives of nations. No man is an island. Each person shares in the collective responsibility of society. No mystical concept of society can be invoked which does not depend on the problems of the individuals of which society is made up. The teaching of Jesus was centred not on vague recommendations for mankind at large, but on specific remedies for the needs of individuals. He had stringent words for the kind of personal rat-race to 'keep up with the Joneses' that is accepted as the norm in our present-day society. 'For everyone who makes himself great will be humbled and whoever humbles himself will be made great.'

As we read through the Gospels, the teaching of Jesus has a most persuasive ring of truth about it. Though the language is different, though the culture is different, he seems to be speaking to us in the twentieth century with a most penetrating relevance to our own problems. His bluntness is devastating; we shrink from it. At the same time his humanity is overwhelming; we are attracted towards it. What he said about man, what he said about society, seems to fit the facts. It seems honest. It appears to be realistic rather than escapist.

Yet it might seem at this point that we are beating our heads against a brick wall. We have seen that the fundamental presuppositions of Christian theism lead to many far-reaching conclusions about the value of man and his significance in the universe. We have seen how the teaching of Christ lays such emphasis on man's importance and his responsibility, and how at the same time the root of evil is in man himself, rather than in his environment. It is also well-known and widely recognized that Jesus' moral and ethical teaching was of the highest quality, and indeed forms the general basis for the moral codes of modern Western civilization.

Have we not simply landed ourselves in an impasse? Even if the ethical teaching of Jesus is so high, what is the point of believing it if we cannot live up to it? Do we not find ourselves in the position of the apostle Paul when he said, 'I don't do the good I want to do, instead, I do the evil that I do not want to do'? If evil is rooted inside man, then what hope can there be of living like Christ? Of course if everyone obeyed the Sermon on the Mount, then the world would be a much better place to live in – but no one can in fact achieve that kind of standard, so what's the point? If poverty, racialism, strife, class-distinction, violence, misuses of science and technology and all the rest of society's problems are in the long run finally traceable to the selfishness of man, then surely the ethical teaching of Jesus is just showing that selfishness up, rather than curing it?

And have not Buddha and Muhammad and countless other religious leaders put forward great ethical teachings? So are we not always back to the same dilemma, that of the poor man on the front cover of *Objections to Humanism*, trying to pull himself up by his own boot-laces? Is mankind's problem not rooted in the fact that he simply cannot seem to put all these ethical principles into practice, otherwise everything would be all right? Are we not in the dilemma of Desmond King-Hele, who writes at the end of his book entitled *The End of the Twentieth Century*, 'If war is avoided, if the hungry are fed, if the rise in population is checked, and the quality of living is improved by curbing pollution and building new towns fit to live in, we might advance to a marvellously fruitful era when the future wonders of science and technology would be exploited for the benefit of all'? Or of the dilemma of Julian Huxley when he writes, 'We, mankind, contain the possibilities of the earth's immense future, and can realize more and more of them on condition that we increase our knowledge and our love'? Is the history of man not the history of one long 'if'? Is the answer not always 'tomorrow, tomorrow'?

At first sight this impasse seems insoluble. But as we continue to read the Gospels we are faced with other extraordinary claims. Suddenly, like the blinding light at the end of a dark tunnel, the full significance of what Jesus was saying bears in upon us.

The real humanity

'Profound thought is difficult to understand. My thought is difficult to understand. Therefore my thought is profound,' wrote Sir Peter Medawar in a recent book called *The Art of the Soluble*. We might apply the same criticism to a number of interpretations of the life of Christ. In fact what Jesus said was blunt and direct. It was particularly clear when he came to explain, not just his ethical teaching, but who he was, and why he had come.

We have already emphasized the deep humanness clearly portrayed for us in the life of Jesus Christ. So it may not surprise us that one of the favourite titles Jesus used of himself was 'Son of man' (the phrase 'Son of' was used in Hebrew instead of an adjective). But for Jesus to take this particular title startled his contemporaries. For it had come to be associated particularly with the famous prophecy in the book of Daniel in the Old Testament looking forward to the coming of a Messiah: 'And behold, with the clouds of heaven there came one like a son of man . . . his dominion is an everlasting dominion.' So when Jesus used the term about himself, was he implying all that the prophecy included – that despite the seeming victory of his enemies and helplessness of his followers, he was ultimately going to triumph and exert authority over every nation and people?

There are also about 150 instances in the Gospels where Jesus clearly calls God his father in an unusually specific and personal way. Certainly in the Old Testament God was known as 'father' in a more general way, as father of the Jewish people. Jesus used the word in a new and much more individual sense. Even when he was still only twelve years old he was referring to God as '*my* Father' – an extraordinary statement for a child brought up in a Jewish culture where even the sacred name of God, *YHWH*, was deemed too holy to be pronounced by human lips.

If hints were not enough, Jesus went on to claim actual equality with his Father. On one occasion he said bluntly: 'The Father and I are one.' It is not surprising that the Jews started to stone him for uttering such blasphemy. In another place Jesus said plainly, 'Whoever has seen me has seen the Father.' In yet another context Jesus claimed that he had always existed, 'Before Abraham was born, "I am".' 'I AM THAT I AM' was the way in which God had revealed himself to Moses in the Old Testament. Jesus was saying that he shared the same eternal quality of God himself. At the end of his ministry Jesus told his followers to baptise disciples 'in the name of the Father and of the Son and of the Holy Spirit' and the word 'name' is singular here, not plural.

There were other more direct ways in which Jesus made clear his equality with God. On a number of occasions he claimed to forgive people their sins, and as the onlookers protested in shocked exasperation, 'Who can forgive sins but God only?' He also received worship from people without any sign of embarrassment or apparent feeling that the worship was being misdirected. Again, he made the extraordinary claim that the evil which he so clearly analysed in others was not even present in himself. Now there is nothing more annoying than someone who makes himself out to be morally superior to ourselves. Our natural inclination is to retort vindictively, at once pointing out the faults which to us seem so obvious. Yet Jesus challenged his Jewish questioners: 'Which one of you can prove that I am guilty of sin?' and no-one cared to answer the question. Even those men who had lived with Christ for several years, sharing in his lifestyle and his poverty with all the pressures of a ministry dominated night and day by the needs of people, were emphatic in their statements that they had never seen any evil in Jesus. Anyone who has ever 'roughed it' with a group of people for any length of time will know just how significant that is. 'There is no sin in him,' states John. Peter described Jesus as 'a lamb without defect or spot', a reference to the Jewish Passover Feast where a sacrificial lamb had to be picked out which was perfect in every detail.

As we read on in the life of Christ we are struck by the fact that Jesus was constantly pointing towards himself as the answer to man's problems, rather than towards his teaching. This is in marked contrast to religious leaders such as Buddha or Muhammad. Gautama the Buddha forsook the luxurious life of a young Kshatriya prince and set out on a wandering ministry to teach people how they could escape from the bondage of desire. But it has been pointed out by H. D. Lewis and R. L. Slater in *World Religions* that 'when Buddha at the time of his death, was asked how it would be best to remember him he simply urged his followers not to trouble themselves about such a question. It did not matter much whether they remembered him or not, the essential thing was the teaching . . .' Similarly Muhammad pointed away from himself towards his teaching. For anyone to claim that he was equal with God or worthy to be worshipped would be the ultimate blasphemy for the Muslim. Yet when we come to Christ we find that he states quite categorically, 'I am the way, I am the truth, I am the life; no one goes to the Father except by me.' In other places he says 'I am the light of the world', 'I am the door', 'I am the good shepherd', 'I am the resurrection and the life' – a whole series of vivid models to express the fact that the key to life was in himself and not just in his teaching. He never said 'My teaching is the life', but 'I am the life'.

It is quite impossible to accept Jesus as simply a religious teacher if we are to do justice to the facts. His egoistic teaching would be overbearing if he was not the person he claimed to be – nothing less than God himself in human flesh. All our attempts to assign Jesus to some neat little list of the 'world's religious leaders', all our efforts to keep him as some comforting religious symbol, or to extract his ethical teaching from his teaching about himself, must surely fail if we are going to take the historical documents seriously. For those who lived with Jesus the light gradually dawned. What he said, coupled with the miracles that he performed and the moral impact of the purity and humanity of his life, eventually led one of the disciples, Peter, to exclaim, 'You are the Messiah, the Son of the living God.' And when Thomas, not the disciple the best known for his ready acceptance of new information, finally met the risen Christ, he blurted out, 'My Lord and my God.'

Near the end of his life the apostle John, who must have pondered deeply over the significance of the life of Christ, used a most expressive model to describe who Jesus was. He said simply that Jesus was the 'Word'. In some ways this is the ultimate model. It is saying that God has spoken, that he has acted in history, that he has torn through the seemingly closed system of our space-time continuum to reveal himself in the only way that our minds could grasp, in the person of Jesus Christ. In Jesus was therefore fully embodied the expression of God. We know what God is like because we know what Jesus was like. We know that God is love because we have watched the unceasing out-going acts of compassion of Jesus of Galilee, a life completely taken up by the needs of others. We know that God is all-powerful and the creator and sustainer of all things by the fact that Jesus with a word calmed a rough sea and exerted power over disease and death. We know that God is holy by the way that Jesus stormed through the Jewish temple with a whip in a whirlwind of passionate righteousness turning out those who would use 'his Father's house' as a place for making money. Jesus is the Word, the language of humanity, the medium through which an infinite God chose to communicate with finite minds.

Jesus was saying that his was the real humanity. This was the way that God had made real human beings to be – not people held in the shackles of their own selfishness, but those who could be released into a new dimension of living. If the first main key to understanding the life of Christ comes in realizing who Jesus was, then the second main key comes in realizing why he came, and, in particular, why he *died*.

The sign of the cross has become such a familiar sight all over the world that it is difficult to disentangle its modern usage from its historical context. For some it has become a dimly recollected symbol which, like a flag, if waved hard enough, will arouse some kind of emotion. For many it is simply a religious ornament worn round the neck. For others it has become an object of devotion, as if the very symbol itself was somehow worthy of worship. For some, the cross has become more like a plus-sign for raking in dollars. Religious business can be big business.

Historically the cross had been used in various countries as an instrument of torture long before the time of Christ. There is evidence of its use in Persia by the sixth century BC, in Egypt by the fifth century BC, and in India, Scythia and Assyria. The Greeks and Romans adopted it from the Phoenicians, and the Latin historian Cicero stresses its extreme cruelty. By the first century of the Christian era it was commonly reserved amongst Jews only for those guilty of idolatry and blasphemy, whilst in the Roman Empire as a whole it was used only for slaves, and citizens were exempt from it. In enemy-occupied Israel it must have been a common occurrence to see small processions of people carrying the *patibulum*, the cross-beam which was fixed to an upright post to form a cross, wending their way out of Jerusalem to the traditional spots for crucifixion outside the city walls. Occasionally there would be crucifixions on a massive scale. In 4 BC the Roman general Varus is reported to have crucified 2,000 Jewish insurgents, and it was the crucifixion of 3,600 Jews by Florus in AD 66 which precipitated the Jewish rebellion. During the siege of Jerusalem by Titus in AD 70 so many were crucified that there was a shortage of wood.

It has often been pointed out that a sizeable proportion of the Gospels is taken up with the events leading up to the crucifixion of Jesus. Why was his death so important? What in fact happened at the cross of Jesus Christ? Was it just the tragic end to an exceptional life? Or a beautiful example of the way in which death should be accepted? Or a kind of dramatic execution of a revolutionary leader, in the style of Che Guevara, whose spirit would live on long after he was dead? Was it just one more execution amongst thousands taking place in Roman-occupied territory where political revolt was simmering never far below the surface?

The New Testament writers are unanimous in rejecting all these suggestions as being the central reason why Jesus died.

Jesus himself had spoken of his coming death as being 'a ransom for many', as a price to be paid for release from slavery. Jesus also applied to himself a prophecy in which the coming Messiah would be a suffering sacrifice taking on himself the grief and alienation of the people. He spoke of his blood being shed 'for the forgiveness of sins'. The apostle Peter wrote afterwards that 'Christ himself carried our sins on his body to the cross, so that we might die to sin and live for righteousness'. John said that 'the blood of Jesus, God's Son, makes us clean from sin'. Paul said that 'God offered Christ so that by his death he should become the means by which men's sins are forgiven, through their faith in him. God offered him to show how he puts men right with himself'. The writer to the Hebrews also emphasizes that the central purpose of Jesus' death was on account of sin: 'He has now appeared once and for all, when all ages of time are now nearing the end, to remove sin through the sacrifice of himself'. And Paul says that 'God was in Christ reconciling the world to himself'.

In other words, in some utterly profound way, Christ was undergoing the punishment and rejection that we deserve. At the cross, all the evil which man is responsible for, and which is rooted in his very nature, was flowing over Jesus in a great overwhelming tide of mental, physical and, above all, spiritual anguish. God himself had entered space and time and was himself personally in Christ accepting the consequences of man's sin, evil, alienation and rejection of him, in one great sacrificial paroxysm of indescribable grief. At the cross Jesus accepted injustice as he was executed instead of Barabbas, the murderer, for as Pilate had said to the crowds, 'I cannot find anything Jesus has done to deserve death'. At the cross it was the innocent who suffered. At the cross there was racialism as the despised 'man of Galilee' was trodden under the heel of the religio-political establishment. At the cross there was alienation as Jesus' own close friends and family watched him die. At the cross there was all the pompous pride and selfishness of a group of men who were afraid to see their power structure shaken. At the cross there was jealousy as the ineffectuality of a dry moralistic system was shown up for what it really was. At the cross there was the crude cynicism of those who mocked and jeered and felt that their little world view seemed secure after all. At the cross there was a man who did not seem to care about standing on his rights. Finally, in that great cry of dereliction, 'My God, my God, why did you forsake me', Jesus expressed that separation which in some deeply mysterious way entered the personal relationship of the Trinity itself as God took on himself the evil of a world which seemed intent on destroying him. As one of the men who watched him die later put it: 'This is what love is: it is not that we have loved God, but that he loved us and sent his son to be the means by which our sins are forgiven.'

The New Testament writers saw the word 'sin' not in the half-amused, slightly cynical way in which it has come to be used in our culture as a kind of blanket term for sexual deviations, but rather as a useful summary word to describe that whole attitude of mind which prefers to place self at the centre of life rather than God. Sin was not therefore referring so much to specific wrongs as to the basic problem of man's evil which separates him from God. Sin means missing-out on the kind of life that God really wants us to enjoy. It is expressed in that determination to live our own lives that results in a yawning chasm which separates man from a holy God. As the holiness of God was revealed in Jesus Christ we realize that our own lives could never measure up to that holiness, that blinding purity. Man was created to know God, but it would seem an impossibility. No evil could stand in the presence of the utter holiness of God. And God could not deny his own nature by simply wishing it away. So it is our evil, our self-centredness, our own turning away from God, which keeps us from him. If he seems so very far away to twentieth-century man, it is not his fault. It is entirely ours.

This is why the New Testament writers saw the cross as so deeply significant. As Jesus went down into death, so he took man's evil with him. He bore the penalty of alienation from God which sin inevitably brings. As Jesus died, the great curtain of the

Jewish temple in Jerusalem, which separated the ordinary people from the symbolic presence of God, tore in two from top to bottom. As Jesus died it was as if a way had been opened up for the ordinary man into the very presence of God himself. All the barriers had been shattered.

But it was not only the barriers to a true knowledge of God which were being shattered, but the very grip of death itself. Within a few days of the crucifixion the whole of Jerusalem was buzzing with a new scandal. Jesus had risen! The Jews quickly put round a rumour suggesting that the body had been stolen. But the facts were too persuasive. About twenty years afterwards it was recorded in one document that over five hundred people had seen Jesus after his resurrection, most of whom were still alive at the time the letter was written. Within a few weeks of the resurrection a bunch of rather timid disciples had been transformed into a kind of revolutionary task-force proclaiming boldly on the streets and in the market-places that Jesus was not only alive, but had completely turned their lives upside down, so much so that some of the crowds thought they were drunk!

Now as with the other miracles, our attitude towards the evidence for the resurrection will depend entirely on how much we allow the cultural soaking of Rationalism to effect our presuppositions, and how much we are willing to admit at least the possibility of Christian theism. If we are willing to admit the possibility, then at least we will be open to the further possibility that the resurrection *could* happen. Once we have opened our minds to that extent, then we will be ready to study the historical evidence to find out whether it in fact *did* happen. Clearly if the resurrection did happen, then it would certainly fit with who Jesus said he was; if he was really God revealed as a human 'model', then we would hardly expect him to be limited by death.

All the documents that we have are careful to point out that they were talking in terms of a literal bodily resurrection of Jesus Christ. After the resurrection the tomb was empty in contrast to the situation a few minutes earlier when there had been a body in it. The risen Jesus was no ethereal ghost, but one who still had a recognizable body. He could talk, drink and eat meat. There is no hint that the documents were just referring to a kind of vague continuation of the ideas of Jesus in the minds of the disciples. They were not saying that the disciples had just made an existential commitment to a person who had made a great impression on them, but who was still dead. The account has no parallels with a kind of Greek legendary figure who rises again every year in a cyclical pattern of re-birth. The New Testament documents are telling us that Jesus died once historically and rose once historically. 'If Christ has not been raised,' said Paul, writing to the Christians at Corinth, 'then your faith is a delusion and you are still lost in your sins.'

Even for a scientist who is naturally sceptical of anything abnormal, the evidence for the resurrection does indeed seem very convincing. Of course there is no such thing as 'proof' when we come to historical events. Even in the most recently recorded history, we are still dependent on the evidence of eye-witnesses. The important factor is to weigh the evidence and try to place the event within the historical and cultural framework of the times. There have been a number of popular recent books surveying the evidence in this way, such as *Man Alive*! by Michael Green, *Who Moved the Stone?* by Frank Morison and *The Davidson Affair* by Stuart Jackman. So we shall not need to go into it here. Professor J. N. D. Anderson, Professor of Oriental Law and Director of the Institute of Advanced Legal Studies in the University of London, has written of the 'overwhelming' evidence for the resurrection he finds in studying the documentary evidence from a legal point of view.

If the resurrection is true, everything is changed. First, it is the final confirmation that Jesus was who he said he was. As Jesus burst from the tomb he was proclaiming that death had no hold on him, that even the full weight of man's evil could not keep him there, that now a new humanity was possible which would not be shackled by the problems of its own selfishness. He was saying that the bridge between man and God had been completed, that 'a new and living way' had been opened up for man to have personal knowledge of a personal God. The whole problem of evil had been dealt with once and for all in that one decisive, traumatic sacrifice of self-giving. When Jesus ascended to be with his Father he was saying that his new resurrection body was quite outside the limits of space and time, though it could be expressed within those limits, as in the post-resurrection appearances. He was saying that he could now act as a direct personal link between man and God, so that a living fellowship with God could become a possibility for all men.

But, more than this, Jesus had already told his disciples before his death and resurrection that after his ascension he would send his Spirit, who would represent his continuing activity on earth. In fact Jesus had even said that it would be to their advantage when the Holy Spirit came because his Spirit would actually live out his life through them. It would be just as if Jesus himself was living inside them, clothing them with his power and humanity Historically it was at Pentecost that this in fact happened. Within a few weeks of the Holy Spirit filling the twelve disciples with the very dynamism and power of God himself, thousands had believed in Christ and experienced the same transformation. Within a few hundred years of Pentecost, churches had sprung up all over the Middle East, North Africa, Europe, and some had even started in India, until finally, after centuries of persecution, Christianity was accepted officially into the Roman Empire itself.

The message of the early church was simple and direct. God had acted in history. In the Old Testament he had revealed his laws to the Jewish people. Because of the basic problem of sin and evil they had been unable to keep those laws. The law in itself was morally excellent, but it had the practical effect of exposing man's problems rather than solving them. God had taught the Jews a system of sacrifices which emphasized their dependence on him, and the fact that sin could not simply be overlooked. The ministry and mission of a Messiah who would deliver them from this bondage had been predicted by the Old Testament prophets. This had now found its fulfilment in Jesus Christ.

Jesus, in his life and teaching, had fulfilled the law in every detail. He was therefore the only truly human being who had ever lived. He was the only one who had completely fulfilled God's creative plan for man. He was the only one who had ever lived in complete harmony and sinlessness towards both God, his fellow men and himself. In this sense he was the representative of man. But while he was truly human, he was also truly divine. He was the son of God himself. So Jesus, in his death, had taken the 'curse of the law' on himself. He died the death of all those who were to be united with him by faith. He rose from death to make it possible for them to share his new life too. The Holy Spirit of Christ would re-motivate and re-make all those who were willing to look to Jesus as the only solution to the problem of evil. When Christ had been willingly accepted into the life in this way, then he would share his life with the recipient. He would begin to spread his love in that person's heart; he would share his joy and peace; he would give a new direction and purpose to life; he would give power to overcome evil; he would re-orientate the person towards God where formerly he had been turned in on self.

To come into this new life of personal fellowship with God, the early church proclaimed that two vital steps were necessary. The first was repentance, the second faith.

The last thing that most people want to do is repent. It involves accepting that we have a real responsibility for our actions. It means admitting that God is right, and that we are wrong. An essential part is the realization of what our life is really like when we measure it up against the holiness of God and the true humanity of Jesus Christ. It means realizing that we have fallen short of the sort of human being that God intended us to be, and that our very self-centredness is what is separating us from personal knowledge of a holy God. In repentance we therefore deliberately turn from our old life towards God and the kind of life that he wants us to experience. It involves a complete willingness to be ready for the plan and purpose that God has for our lives.

Repentance is difficult because it involves a blow to our pride.

This is why Jesus reserved his most caustic comments for those whose pride prevented them from seeing their own need. Yet how else could we approach God? Look up into the heavens on a clear summer's night. Remind yourself that each solar system, each star, the angle of the earth as it rotates on its axis, each animal and tree, the atoms of your body and the air you breathe – all this is sustained by the active creativity of a personal God. Then think of the moral purity of the revelation of God in Jesus Christ. How else could we come to God than through a recognition of our own creatureliness, our own pathetic self-assertion, our own moral pollution?

But it is not repentance alone which makes us a Christian. The second essential step is faith. Unfortunately the word faith has often a quite different meaning in our modern usage from the way it was used in the New Testament. Due partly to the influence of existentialist philosophy, the word 'faith' has come to have the connotation of a blind leap in the dark, a commitment to something without being very clear as to the object or aim of the commitment. The emphasis is therefore placed on the faith itself rather than on the object of that faith. We have already used the word 'faith' in its more existential sense whilst discussing various blind 'leaps of faith' made by those attempting in philosophical or experimental ways to find their way out of the dilemma of 'man in the box'.

For the New Testament writers faith was a way *into* something rather than a way *out of* something. It was not an escape from a difficult intellectual situation, but the logical result of facing up to the facts about the life, death and resurrection of Jesus Christ. The essence of their use of the word could be summed up in our word 'trust'. They were challenging people to enter into a personal relationship with God through Jesus Christ, a relationship of trust in him, trusting too in what Christ had done for them in his death. Jesus was to be placed at the centre of their lives and made Lord now, not self.

Faith was a natural response to who Jesus was. It showed a complete willingness to allow the sort of life Jesus had taught about, the life of Jesus himself, to be lived out through them. So far-reaching were the results in people's lives and their impact on society that when the first Christians reached Thessalonica in Greece, the local crowds attacked them saying that 'These men who have turned the world upside down have come here also.' Paul described the experience by saying that 'If any one is in Christ, he is a new creation, the old has passed away, behold the new has come.' Jesus himself had earlier said that the step was such a fundamental one that it was like being born all over again and having a completely new life. Peter makes the same point when he writes that 'Because of God's great mercy, he gave us new life by raising Jesus Christ from the dead.'

Since the Day of Pentecost millions of people have experienced that same personal relationship with the same personal, infinite God, through the same pathway of repentance and faith. The way is basically identical for all men. The cross is the great social leveller. Salvation depends not on the colour of our skin, nor on the quality of our genes, nor on how moral we are, nor on whether we go to church or have gone through some catechism, nor on our intelligence or intellectual ability or status in society. It depends simply on whether we are willing to recognize that we cannot solve the problem brought about by our own evil and selfishness by ourselves, and whether we are willing in the light of this to place our trust in Jesus Christ and start living for him instead of ourselves.

A personal relationship to God through Jesus Christ in this way is no new mysticism. The essence of a mystical experience, as we have already noted, is that it has no propositional content which can be communicated by words. It is rooted in an escape from reason. The mystic is one who believes (to quote *Webster's Dictionary*) that a direct knowledge of God or spiritual truth or ultimate reality is attainable 'through immediate intuition or insight and in a way differing from ordinary sense perception or the use of logical reasoning.' Or, as Alan Richardson puts it in *A Dictionary of Christian Theology*, the mystic turns 'inwards on his own consciousness and experience, and by stressing the necessity for discarding from his mind all visual or concrete images, comes to realize in a peculiarly coercive way his essential oneness with ultimate reality.'

The personal relationship with God that may be experienced through Jesus Christ is not mystical in this sense, but rather a rationally-based response to Jesus Christ, who rose from the dead as a historical fact, and who is thus alive, if not now in our own world of sense-perception. The revelation of God in Christ is accepted because, as a general model of explanation, it 'fits the facts' about the human condition in a way that no other model does.

So this new relationship is no more or less mystical than any other personal relationship. When we know a person it is quite a different thing from knowing *about* a person. When we know about a person then we could state certain objective propositional statements about the person which we believe to be true. We might liken this to an intellectual knowledge about the character of God. But once we know the person then there is a complex interplay of objective and subjective factors which make up the relationship. It is as if there were a continuum between two opposite poles of objectivity and subjectivity. The relationship touches that continuum at every point. At one end of the scale we can still make objective statements about the person which are demonstrably true. At the other end of the scale we can only say that we *know* the person, and that if someone else wants to know what he is really like, then he must come and meet him too. In that sense, personal encounter is the only way to know a person. Once the encounter has taken place, then we can say with absolute certainty and complete reasonableness that we know the person, even though there is no kind of scientific or mathematical 'proof' that could demonstrate the point within those frameworks of reference. If we want to describe as 'mystical' every element of personal knowledge which engendered this kind of certainty, then we could indeed call a personal knowledge of Christ 'mystical', but in this case we would be going a long way beyond the way in which the world is normally used.

A personal knowledge of God, a trust in God, is therefore essentially non-mystical; indeed it has the most mundane, down-to-earth, practical results in our everyday lives. But at the same time it is most certainly transcendental in the sense that we can know a relationship with a transcendent God who is the ultimate source of everything that exists and who cannot possibly be encompassed within the puny limits of our minds. In this way our deepest subjective longing for the transcendent and the 'beyond', which God has created us to experience, finds its fulfilment in him.

This personal knowledge of God is at the same time most decidedly supernatural. There is no question of it being simply a process of personal reform, a programme of self-help or turning over a new leaf, an attempt to align ourselves according to the ethics of Christ, or a good resolution to make a greater moral effort. No, it is the living God himself coming into our lives as we invite him to do so, and changing us through his own life-giving creative power.

At the same time coming to know Christ personally is not like swallowing some pill which will then solve all our problems. It represents no magic potion whereby we are instantly changed into some kind of 'moral superman'. Knowing God in our lives has all the characteristics of any other relationship. Our person-alities are not erased, rather they are liberated into a new freedom. Our genes remain the same. If we had a crooked nose before, then it will still be crooked afterwards. The New Testament writers saw coming to Christ as rather like joining a family. It was a family where the people were all different, but where they all had one thing in common – they all shared the same new life in Christ. Becoming a Christian might therefore be likened to the analogy of a wedding where a relationship is sealed by saying 'I will' on a certain day. That act of the will is not the end of the matter, but the beginning. Afterwards the marriage relationship will continue to grow, and there will be that changing kaleido-scopic pattern of joys, trials, hopes, happiness and fulfilment which are all part and parcel of sharing one's life with another.

Being a Christian is a dynamic, growing relationship, in which our life is daily shared with the living Lord Jesus Christ.

It seems extraordinary, especially to one living in a 'post-Christian culture', that some should think that becoming a Christian is just a process of wishful thinking. Those who do not want to face up to the evidence for Christian belief might indeed be facing a problem of 'wishful non-thinking'. So deeply is our culture soaked with non-Christian presuppositions, that it is only by a definite effort of will that we can wrest our minds from the whole framework of reference with which we have been presented since birth, and consider the possibility that the framework might just happen not to be true. To do this requires a considerable intellectual honesty and a willingness at least to expose ourselves to the evidence which is available. Wading against a strong cultural current is not an easy thing to do.

At the same time, for those who find a new, real humanity in Jesus Christ, there are many far-reaching implications which touch every area of their lives. Since God is the God of the whole universe, of everything that is, it is hardly surprising that knowing him changes everything. Neither are those changes necessarily easy to implement. The way of the cross is a costly way, as well as a way of joyful fulfilment. Just what this way involves in terms of man and society, and science and the drift from science, we must now go on to consider.

Chapter Five

THE NEW CREATION

D. H. Lawrence once wrote that there was no kind of inspiration which could get 'weak, impotent, vicious, worthless and rebellious man' beyond his limits, and that therefore Christ's Christianity was doomed to failure. If Lawrence was saying that no one could live up to the standards that Christ set, then there is no doubt that he was right. But we have seen that real Christianity is not a question of trying to live up to a standard, but of allowing the Lord of creation to enter our lives and clothe us with his real humanity. The Christian is only too aware that this new humanity does not come from himself. At the cross Christ had died his death, his moral impotence had been removed. As C. S. Lewis once put it: 'Jesus has forced open the door that had been locked since the death of the first man. He has met, fought and beaten the King of Death. Everything is different because he has done so. This is the beginning of the New Creation: a new chapter in cosmic history has opened.'

Those individuals who have experienced this new humanity, who have entered into that new creation which comes through repentance and faith in Jesus Christ, find themselves as members of a new community. There is no possible smugness or pride in being part of that new community. They realize that the source of their new life is Jesus, who once called himself the 'bread of life'. When they share that new life with others, they feel like a beggar telling another beggar where he can find bread.

In the new community all the old barriers are broken down. As Paul wrote, 'There is no difference between Jews and Gentiles, between slaves and free men, between men and women: you are all one in union with Christ Jesus.' The community is a world-wide community. It surpasses all barriers of race, colour, class, education and political ideology. It is a union of those who have found their humanness in Christ.

The new community is like a task-force, a group of people living out here and now a new order which is still future, the new creation. They experience a real moral and intellectual freedom through knowing Christ, the source of truth. As Jesus once said: 'Everyone who sins is a slave of sin', but 'if the Son makes you free, then you will be really free.' Their moral freedom is not a moral anarchy, nor does it mean perfection, but rather a freedom from the grip of sin on their lives. Sin inevitably means death – but this penalty has already been paid at the cross. Now the power of sin is also broken as the risen Christ enters and lives his life through them. Their intellectual freedom comes through knowing that their God is the God of the whole creation, and there is therefore nothing in any part of it which cannot be explored for fear that it will shake their world-view, whether it be the innermost recesses of the mind or the outermost reaches of space. The whole world is God's world.

The world-wide new community was called by the New Testament the church. It is hardly surprising that this is a word which produces a mental block in many people today. Hardly anything could be further from the revolutionary bands of disciples which began to group themselves after Pentecost and infiltrate society, than some of the moribund, hierarchical, bureaucratic structures which still sometimes pass as 'churches' today. Anyone could be forgiven for being 'turned off' Christianity by such institutions. They are far away from the principles which Jesus so clearly taught. Some insist on the accumulation of vast amounts of wealth, when Jesus said quite clearly to his disciples 'Don't pile up treasures on earth.' Others seem intent on creating hierarchical structures where the emphasis is on the pomp and prestige of leaders, in marked contrast to the simple life-style of Christ, who said that 'Whoever tries to gain his own life will lose it, whoever loses his life for my sake will gain it', and that 'If one of you wants to be great, he must be the servant of the rest; and if one of you wants to be first, he must be your slave . . .'

In the New Testament the churches were gatherings of people who had themselves experienced the new creation, and so sought to teach and live out what Jesus actually said. They adopted the two symbolic practices that Jesus instituted – baptism and communion. They appointed a church leadership responsible for teaching and maintaining the cohesion of the community.

Happily, down the centuries since Pentecost, there have been local communities all over the world whose central aims have been aligned with these same principles. Whenever the revolutionary life of Christ has been allowed to dominate the thinking of both the individuals and the community as a whole, then there has been a renewed emphasis on the basic essentials and a deep impact on the society of which that community is a part. The social impact of one community is seen in the words of Justin Martyr when he addressed the Roman Emperor Antonius Pius in the second century: 'Since our persuasion by the Word . . . we who once used magical arts dedicate ourselves to the good and unbegotten God; we who valued above all things the acquisition of wealth and possessions now bring what we have into a common stock and communicate to everyone in need; we who hated and destroyed one another, and on account of their different manners would not share the same hearth with men of another tribe, now since the coming of Christ live on intimate terms with them, and pray for our enemies and endeavour to persuade those who hate us to live according to the good precepts of Christ, so that they may become partakers with us of the same joyful hope . . .'

Eighteen hundred years later Richard Wurmbrand, who himself suffered fourteen years for his faith in a Rumanian prison, describes in *Tortured for Christ* the kind of impact that a Christian community made in filthy prison cells: 'I have seen Christians in communist prisons with fifty pounds of chains on their feet, tortured with red hot pokers, in whose throats spoonfuls of salt have been forced, being kept afterwards without water, starving, whipped, suffering from cold and praying with fervour for the communists. This is humanly inexplicable! It is the love of Christ which was shed into our hearts . . .' This is the kind of dynamism of God's love which is let loose into society through any community which is taking Christ's teaching seriously. As one American hippie put it, when he became a Christian: 'Jesus Christ has given me a love for radicals whose ideologies are different from mine.'

Those communities which are truly churches in the New Testament sense of the word are not limited to any one single denomination or organization. Rather they are scattered all over the world throughout the various denominations. It is not the label which matters, but the people. The community might meet in all shapes and sizes of buildings, from a cathedral to a coal-cellar. Some might meet in ultra-modern buildings, some in the living-room of a local house, some, facing the oppression of totalitarian states, out in the woods for fear of being found out. The place is irrelevant; it is the people who represent the new creation.

The marks of such communities are the same wherever they are found in the world: humanity, warmth, acceptance, love, communication, a desire to serve, a proclamation of what Jesus really said, a longing for others to share in this new creation. No community is perfect; each one has its faults. But the marks of a true New Testament community shine through the imperfections. Where such a group exists, people are attracted. A recent survey of churches in the London area showed that people were being drawn largely to those churches where historic Christian belief was being both practised and preached. Those where a watered-down message was being presented had few people. Nominal church attendance may be on the decline, but those communities which bear the characteristics of a New Testament church continue to attract large numbers. At the same time there is a great world-wide movement towards Jesus Christ, chiefly among students and young people, often expressed in a context quite outside the traditional denominations. The Jesus Movement has attracted wide publicity. Not so well known is the fact that hundreds each year are becoming Christians in universities and colleges as an increasing number of people become disillusioned with the inconsistencies of materialistic answers.

Of course historically much has passed for Christianity which is nothing of the kind. As Jesus once said, the kingdom of God is like a big tree, and sometimes a lot of strange birds are found sheltering in its branches. If the early Christians had been able to watch newsreels of the Crusades, the Thirty Years War, the Spanish Inquisition and Northern Ireland, they would have been startled at the suggestion that such things could possibly be done in the name of Christianity. As one of the disciples put it, 'Whoever does not love does not know God, because God is love . . . If someone says "I love God" yet hates his brother, he is a liar.' But if further newsreels had been shown of William Wilberforce battling against the slave-trade, of Lord Shaftesbury fighting in Parliament for better conditions for factory-workers, of Dr Barnardo founding homes for orphans, of Christian doctors starting leper colonies in Thailand, of Christian relief agencies getting involved in the Pakistani refugee problem in India, then they would have immediately recognized such actions as stemming from a real Christian faith which had accepted the radically new humanity of Jesus Christ. Perhaps one of the saddest dates in Christian history was when Christianity became the official religion of the Roman Empire, and millions started calling themselves 'Christians' for the purpose of toeing the party line. Fortunately today that tide of 'official Christianity', which has often been no more than one of the pawns (if not a bishop) in the games of international politics, is gradually receding, leaving those communities of people who believe in New Testament Christianity standing out like rocks at low tide.

The long-term effect of using the word 'Christian' in its vague official sense, rather than its authentic Biblical sense, has been that for many the word has ceased to have any real meaning. By the criteria of linguistic analysis it has almost become a nonsense word. If the word 'Christian' as a description was applied to everyone who claimed that they were one, then it would include a mixed group of people, largely deist, some agnostic, a few atheist, with a scattering of theists. The word used in this sense would lose any power whatsoever to describe a particular group of people. Fortunately there is now a move to use it only in its original sense of referring to those who have had a personal life-changing trust in Jesus Christ.

One of the functions of the new community is that they are a worshipping body. Their aim in life is to give glory to God, something which has to be worked out at every level of their lives. Another function is that they are a witnessing body, which involves communicating what God has done for them both verbally and in the character of their lives. In communal worshipping and witnessing they experience something of what true living can and will be like. A worshipping community is a sharing community. The mask which a materialistic society tends to force upon them can be left behind at the cross. They can afford to be real people, not plastic people. At the same time there is the tension which comes from the overlap of two ages. They are the new creation, but at the same time the old creation is very much alive.

One of the signs of the passage from the old creation to the new creation is baptism. In the New Testament this is pictured as being rather like a burial. Just as Christ went down into the grave, so the person being baptised goes down into the water. As Christ was raised from the dead, so the person comes out of the water. This dramatizes what happens when a person repents and believes, and so identifies himself with the death and resurrection of Jesus. His old life has been left behind and buried at the cross. The water is a symbol that his sins have been washed away through Christ's sacrifice. He rises again, so to speak, in the newness of life that Christ gives through his Spirit.

Holy Communion, or the 'breaking of bread' as it was commonly called in the early church, is another cohesive force in the new community, as it repeats the same symbolism in the regular life of the church. It looks back to the beginning of the new creation. As a memorial feast it commemorates the fact of Christ's historical death. The simple symbols of bread and wine reflect the grass-roots involvement of the new community in the everyday world of things. There is nothing mystical about either symbol; they were the ordinary things of first-century meal-tables. At the first 'Lord's supper', in the context of the Jewish Passover Feast, Jesus gave the bread and the wine to his disciples with the words, 'Do this in memory of me.' The wine is a vivid reminder of the blood of Christ which was shed in his sacrificial death. The tearing of the bread symbolizes that world-changing moment when the God of the whole universe took, in Christ, the consequences of our evil nature upon himself. But the breaking of bread is a feast of joy. It is a liberating feast. The claims of sin, the shackles of our old lives, have gone. It is also a feast which looks forward eagerly to the time when Jesus is going to return, this time in his full power and glory, unrestricted by the limitations of a physical body, and restore the whole of creation to the normality which it has never experienced since the fall of man.

The new community therefore finds itself as a forerunner of God's restoration of his creation to a true normality. Evil has left a deep scar across the universe, the whole of creation has been affected. Nothing is normal. The cross of Christ has a cosmic significance because it was there that the power of evil was crushed. Nothing can be the same again. The seeds of the new creation have been sown in the lives of those who have trusted in Christ. The culmination and complete fulfilment of that new creation will not occur until Christ comes again. In that day there will be a 'new heaven and a new earth'.

The task of the new community is therefore to bring healing to a world scarred by evil. The healing will never be complete because not all men will come to the source of the new creation, Christ himself. It is as if the world is gripped by a cancer of evil; only a proportion of the cells of each affected tissue can be restored to normal function. Complete healing and relief from malignancy would be possible only with the total restoration of each cell. Jesus said this was impossible before his coming again because many would choose to reject him. He never suggested that the kingdom of God was something which could be built on earth by man's own effort. Everywhere Jesus went he preached the 'good news of the kingdom'. He was not referring to some kind of utopian dream, but a new reality which was even then breaking in on the old through his own person and ministry. To his listeners at one point he said that 'in fact the kingdom of God is among you', and in another place that through his power 'the kingdom of God has already come upon you'. The secret of belonging to the kingdom lay in belonging to him. There was no way of earning membership by trying to be moral; it involved personal faith in him.

God's kingdom was therefore to consist of that new community of people who had made Jesus 'king', or ruler, of their lives. At the same time they were to realize that the kingdom would find its final consummation only when Christ came again. Until that time the primary task of the new community should be to bring others into that kingdom through their worship and witness. As Jesus said, 'This good news about the kingdom will be preached through all the world, for a witness to all mankind – and then will come the end.' Until people were brought into a personal relationship with God, they had not even discovered their *raison d'être*, they had not started to live. They were not normal people. As Stephen Neill has put it: 'A man is only a man when he is like God and lives in fellowship with him.' Coming to know God was the starting-point, because it was at that point that a man was restored to his natural state, that he was brought back to some degree of normality. So the fundamental task of the new community was to bring men to God so that the natural pattern and purpose of their lives, which had been spoilt by evil, should be restored. At the same time they should be like 'salt to the world'. Salt in the time of Christ was valued as a preservative and for seasoning food. It was often used among Oriental peoples for ratifying agreements, so that it became a symbol of honesty. The new community should therefore have a substantial healing effect upon society. Every part of God's creation would be affected, at physical, moral and social levels.

The pilot-plant

Dr Francis Schaeffer, in *Pollution: A Christian View of Ecology*, has likened the new community to a kind of 'pilot-plant'. Before a complete factory is established, a pilot-plant is set up which reproduces in miniature the aims and goals of the complete factory which is ultimately envisaged. The pilot-plant only finds its complete fulfilment in the factory, but meanwhile it can accomplish something: it can mirror the greater reality which is yet to come. So the new community is like a pilot-plant whose aim is to produce on earth at least a recognizable reflection of what God is going to accomplish ultimately, after the second coming of Christ, in his creation of the new heavens and new earth.

The pilot-plant has no illusion about its limitations. It realizes that it is not the factory itself. It is not utopian, for it recognizes the continuing power of evil in the world as there is a continuing rejection of God's new creation in Christ. But it has a real basis for its action, it has a definite framework of reference, it has clear guide-lines for the directions that its actions should take. It is not suggesting the abnormal, but the restoration of the world to the beginning of normality. It does not protest for the sake of protesting, but so that man should adopt what is really natural for him, that role in nature and society which God originally created him to fulfil.

Nature itself has been given to man in trust by God. In the beginning man was given dominion by God over it, and at the same time was told to care for it and treat it as something made by God himself. He was therefore to be a steward of what God had entrusted to him. But as his relationship with God was broken, so he was estranged from his fellow men and from nature itself. As the prophet Jeremiah put it, 'Your wrongdoing has upset nature's order, and your sins have kept you from her kindly gifts.' The long-term results of this estrangement we now see in today's 'eco-crisis'.

So many words have been poured out about pollution, especially since European Conservation Year in 1970, that many

G

people feel themselves almost submerged in an overwhelming wave of statistics, but without any clear idea as to what the basis of their concern is supposed to be. In November 1971 twenty-three industrial plants were closed down indefinitely in Birmingham, Alabama, because air pollution in the city rose to twice the acceptable limit. Every year 142 million tons of smoke and fumes – over 1,400 pounds per head – are released into the air in the United States. A single Sunday edition of the *New York Times* uses 150 acres of forest. In Brazil about 40 per cent of the forests have been cleared within the last 25 years. During the last 2,000 years about 100 different kinds of mammal have become extinct, but the rate of extinction at the moment is about one species per year. In the Baltic sea DDT levels have reached such heights that it is dangerous to eat certain fish from it regularly. Lord Ritchie-Calder has suggested that if the consumption of fossil fuels continues at the present rate, the temperature of the earth might increase by 3.6°C in the next half-century, leading to melting of polar ice and catastrophic flooding. In 1920, 360 million people lived in cities, but this is expected to reach 3,000 million by the year 2000. At present at least 1,000 million people suffer from some form of malnutrition . . .

And so the woeful list goes on. Clearly we have made a mess of our environment. But the depth of our concern seems to be governed by the extent to which the mess is thrown directly back in our own faces. It is not so much the poverty of the world's hungry people that has brought home to us the need for action, as the irritations of which our own prosperity has made us aware. When our favourite beach is spoilt through oil pollution, or the river opposite our house is covered in industrial foam, or oysters are off the menu because the oyster-beds have been polluted, or a new motorway is going to be blasted through the woods half-a-mile away, then we become concerned. But when we hear about forests in another country being devastated to bring us the morning paper, or thousands going to bed hungry because of the wrong use of land, or of fish dying off hundreds of miles away, then somehow we are left cold, because these are not things that seem to affect us directly. As *The Ecologist* of August 1970 had the courage to admit: 'Behind all this is our system of values, the panoply of our expectations and ideals. Obviously, something is wrong with them and they must be changed.' The reasons for pollution are materialistic reasons, and the reasons for our reaction against it are also materialistic reasons. It is debatable therefore whether the fight against pollution on these premises is likely to go any further than our own selfish desire to maintain the prosperity and habitability of our own particular little corner of the world.

Neither can a suitable answer be found to the problem by reacting against materialism towards mysticism. I may well have a mystical feeling that nature is valuable, but there is no particular reason why anyone else should be expected to share the same feelings. As we discussed in chapter two, nor do pantheistic ideas give any basis for seeing any real value in nature, or any reason why we should not treat nature as our own personal impulses might dictate. Nor is there any rational basis for projecting our feelings of sentimentality into non-human things. A tree may be a very nice tree, it may be a very noble tree, but the fact remains that it does not suffer any pain when we cut it down.

The pilot-plant of the new community has a reasonable basis for action because it sees material things as made by God, and therefore good and beautiful and to be enjoyed. The beauty and the enjoyment only cease when those material things are used for selfish ends. Man does have dominion over nature, but he must exert that dominion responsibly. Nature itself is beautiful and should be kept beautiful for its own sake. A tree has value, not because of our feelings injected into it, but simply because of its own tree-ness, the fact that it is something good and unique because created by God. A beautiful vista of mountains and lakes should be preserved as far as possible just because it is part of God's plan to give man pleasure through what is beautiful. The pleasure is not a selfish pleasure because it is willing to return gratitude to the One who made it.

As man is the only one made in God's image, he nevertheless

has a value which is on quite a different scale from the rest of creation. He has an ultimate value. He is far more valuable than any sacred cow. Far more energy should be exerted over the needs of hungry men than the hunger of stray cats. When there is no basis held for the value of man, often choices are made on the basis of sentimentality. The needs of man should never be subjugated to the needs of nature.

One of the functions of the pilot-plant is therefore to bring substantial healing to the nature which has been ravished by man's selfishness and limited world-view. Part of this restoration must be seen in all the other aspects of the environment, in architecture, in town-planning and in art as a whole, in painting, music, sculpture, poetry and literature. In all these the pilot-plant will be concerned to emphasize the humanity and value of man, and his role in creation as a steward of God's goodness. In architecture there will be concern not to de-humanize man by placing him in 'little boxes' or soulless concrete community areas with no sense of a human community at all, but rather to vary and beautify and 'humanize' the environment, even if it is in economically simple ways. In art there will be a desire to express man as he really is, an attempt to tell the truth about the universe, a longing to restore real beauty. There will be an appreciation of the honesty of those who hold different world-views who present man as being non-man and the world as being meaningless, and perhaps do so with great technical skill and ability. Yet simultaneously there will be a shout of protest at the ugliness of the world-view which reduces man to such distortions of his real nature.

The pilot-plant will also be seeking to restore freedom in every possible way. It acts against every attempt to reduce people to pawns in the power-games of politics. People must be listened to just because they are people, because they are important. If left-wing groups shout down people so they cannot be heard, then the pilot-plant is against left-wing groups, in this particular instance. If right-wing groups do the same, then it is against them for the same reason. The value of the individual comes first because he is important because he is made in the image of God, however distorted that image might have become. The pilot-plant will often transcend political parties and boundaries because its world-view may not be rooted in the programmes of any one of them.

Because the pilot-plant places such emphasis and value on each individual person, rather than the more vague needs of movements, programmes and ideals, there will be a fight to feed, heal and bring comfort to the world's sick and hungry. People in the new community do not of course have a monopoly of human compassion; on the other hand their concern does stem directly from their world-view and a love that flows from a personal relationship with their Creator which is not generated by their own efforts. It is a fact that vast amounts of Christian medical, educational and social work have been and are being carried out all over the world. In many cases the benefits of Western medicine have been first brought to a country by Christian doctors and nurses and, following such beginnings, government medical services have grown up alongside these medical missions. One of the big problems all over the world now is the concentration of doctors in the cities rather than in rural areas. In most cases the reasons are obvious – more comfort, security and better hospital amenities in the cities. Those in the new community will be willing to share their humanity with people wherever they are found. In fact, as Dr S. Browne, Director of the Leprosy Study Centre in London, reports, 'The majority of mission hospitals are serving precisely those scattered rural populations which otherwise would be deprived of all medical help.'

Another function of the pilot-plant is the restoration of the family to the kind of pattern and function that God designed it to have. One part of this restoration is in the reinstatement of the parents to the roles that God intended for them. There is one world, which is God's world, and there is one truth, which is God's truth, so we should expect that problems will inevitably come when the creative pattern is destroyed. This is in fact the case.

For example it is well known psychologically that for the normal psychosexual development of a boy in a family, and the development of his sense of what it means to be a man, it is a great help for him to have a good identification with his father. For this identification to occur there should be a prolonged association between father and child in which there is a warm affectionate relationship. There may be many adverse effects on the child if there is a prolonged separation from the father, such as through desertion, or if the father has certain defects of character. Some of the clear-cut syndromes which have been studied in such children are homosexuality, schizophrenia, sexual promiscuity, delinquency and the personal disorders underlying alcoholism or drug addiction.

The main characteristics which run through the descriptions of the fathers of such children is that they tend to be weak or effeminate, and often show a lack of interest in the child leading to little contact and hardly any discipline. In one study, absence of the father in childhood was strongly related to antisocial behaviour among university students.

Now in the revelation of God as 'Father' that we have in Biblical theism there is a model of what the father really should be. It is an interesting fact that in this model lies just those qualities which are lacking in the human father who produces the kind of problems in his children which are mentioned above. The action of the pilot-plant is therefore directed towards restoring the idea of fatherhood to normality. For example in Jesus' parable of the prodigal son there is a beautiful picture of a warm compassionate father. Yet at the same time God the Father is revealed as having authority; he is most definitely not effeminate in character. He is both holy and affectionate. The only full way whereby this true model of fatherhood can be reinstated is through the lives of individuals who come into a personal relationship with God the Father himself. But in a general way the model should be emphasized in society simply because its practise would save so many from emotional and psychological disturbances.

In a similar way the new community fights to restore sex to its full place in God's creative pattern. For the Christian, sex is beautiful because it is made by God. It is made by God for the purposes of reproduction, personal enjoyment, and as a means for both expressing and sealing the love within a marriage relationship. Jesus said clearly that it should not be spoilt by use outside the stable relationship of marriage. Only within the marriage bond is there sufficient security, especially important for the woman, for long-term sexual satisfaction. That security comes not only through two people agreeing to live together, but by their joint vows to each other in some kind of ceremony which is witnessed and accepted by the society of which they are a part. This is no empty charade, but the crucial sociological fact of realizing that no man is an island, and that what two people decide to do has a whole ripple of effects which influence other parts of society. They are not just selfishly opting out of their responsibility to society, but accepting the fact that they are a part of it.

For the Christian, love includes the physical, but is more than the physical. It is only one part of the self-giving to the other person which should mark the marriage relationship. It is no mystical escape from a world of harsh facts, but a natural reflection of the love which has been created into the universe itself by a loving God.

The new community will therefore fight any view of sex which reduces its beauty and which has the effect of de-humanizing men and making sex into little more than an animal experience. The whole trend today seems to be in the direction of depersonalizing love. Antonioni's film *Blow-up* was advertised as 'Murder without guilt, love without meaning'. The female body continues to become increasingly an advertiser's machine for attracting attention to his products, or a bait used to drag people into rather dull theatre productions. Even as sex is made into a god, it tends to reduce both itself, and its worshippers, to nothing.

If all truth is God's truth, then again we would expect to find that when his creative pattern of sex as finding its true fulfilment within marriage breaks down, and when the marriage relationship itself begins to disintegrate increasingly, then there will be definite effects which can be measured in physical, psychological and social terms. Once again, this is in fact what we do find.

Psychologically, if you have sexual relations with several people, your ability to give yourself to any one of them is decreased. A girl will carry on sleeping with someone because she is afraid that otherwise she will lose him, so love becomes distorted by fear. There is uncertainty and mistrust. No amount of correct sexual techniques can replace qualities such as love, integrity and trust. Often the results of 'sleeping around' are loss of self-respect and emotional problems. In later life there can be problems in adjusting sexually to the more stable relationship of marriage. As a London psychiatrist Anthony Storr has written, 'Sex can become a God, and often does so; and a great deal of psychotherapeutic work with people of middle age is concerned with the withdrawal of the projection of the god image from sexuality.'

The increasing breakdown of marriage is having clearly measurable effects on society. About 12 million of the 45 million children in the United States do not live with both parents. The incidence of juvenile delinquency and psychiatric illness is clearly higher amongst those from broken homes, and a vicious circle is under way whereby those from broken homes are themselves more likely to divorce in later life. Statistics of this sort could be multiplied. Yet the causes of breakdown can in nearly every case be traced back to basic selfishness by one or both partners. The humbling experience of allowing God to become the centre of a marriage is that there is a new oneness, a new moral, intellectual and spiritual unity which gives a great cohesive force to the relationship, coupled with the internal dynamic of God's Spirit which releases power to combat selfishness.

The physical effects of moving away from God's creative pattern for the use of sex have received plenty of recent publicity. Venereal disease has reached epidemic proportions. If a person believes that we are in a closed-system universe and that all morals are relative, and that people are there for the enjoyment that you can get out of them, then he would be perfectly rational in treating VD like the risk of catching flu or crossing the road. But it is hardly surprising that this world-view is being challenged when it leads to as much mental and physical distress as it does today. Somehow man does not seem to function properly when God's creative pattern is discarded. Perhaps this explains why some are turning away from such dehumanizing views of man. The new community has no desire to return to Victorian prudishness. Because sex is beautiful it can be talked about freely as something beautiful. But it is its task to try to replace the ugliness which has become associated with sex with the real beauty that it was created to have.

The same longing for that restoration of man to his real humanity will also mean attacking any attempts to use people as a means to an end, rather than as an end in themselves. The problem with Kant's 'categorical imperative' is that you can always choose to ignore it or deny its existence when it becomes convenient to do so. For instance, when there is a pressing political goal or programme that seems very important, the temptation is always there to use people as tools in fulfilling it. Indeed in a world-view where there is no rational basis why people should have any more value than dandelions, it is often difficult to find any good reason why people should not be used as tools anyway. Calling something an 'imperative' gives the feeling that there must be some very pressing reasons for doing something. In this case the feeling is an illusion, and with a closed system world-view there is in fact no particular reason for doing anything at all. However, when you are face to face with the Creator of the universe, and you find that you, along with everyone else, have been made in his image, even though that image has been so marred by your own selfishness, then you find that there is a good basis for treating people as an end in themselves. For the new community people always matter more than things. They are always more important than goals or programmes.

There is a whole range of pressing social questions to which there are no glib easy answers. The Bible does not give a neat list of headings entitled 'abortion', 'euthanasia', and so on, and then proceed to give simple step-by-step answers. The new community is left with the intellectual challenge of applying the basic principles in a whole range of different situations. But the fact that there are basic principles makes an enormous amount of difference. Once again the first question to be asked is this. Does a certain procedure have the ultimate effect of humanizing or dehumanizing man? Does it lead to a higher view of man as having intrinsic value, or to a lower?

This then is the aim of the new community – to fight for the restoration of man. At every level of society the pilot-plant is therefore concerned with giving at least a taste of the new creation, of seeing a renewal of man and his relationships, of restoring nature, family life, art, theatre, sex, the value of the individual and the quality of life in general to at least some recognizable extent.

Another function of the pilot-plant is the restoration of science.

The God of science

We have already traced some of the underlying reasons for the current drift away from science. One of these reasons is the adoption of a world-view, foreign to the early scientists, which has had the effect of elevating science to a god-like status whereby it is made the arbiter of all things. The result is a closed-system mechanistic universe, with no ultimate meaning, in which man appears to be reduced to nothing. Not surprisingly many react against this materialistic position into various mystical and non-rational attempts to find meaning.

In Christian theism reason is restored to its right place. As for the early scientists, it is seen as stemming from a rational God. Reason is therefore good, providing that it does not lose its basic reference point in God himself. When that happens, when reason becomes autonomous, then it becomes something ultimately self-destructive.

One of the effects of a God-orientated reason is to see man's real humanity, including his subjectivity and emotional life, as also being part of the God-image. His subjectivity is therefore also good because it is a normal part of his humanity. There is no justification for extreme objectivity on the one hand, or extreme subjectivity on the other. The balance of truth is between, or more accurately beyond, the extremes of a logical positivist or existentialist position. When reason finds its true reference point, then the necessity for both these extremes is removed.

The scientist who is a Christian sees the scientific method as neither completely objective nor completely individualistic. He recognizes the value-judgments involved in putting forward and testing scientific theories, but at the same time sees that experiments are reproducible by any scientist anywhere in the world providing that the number of variables is kept reasonably small and the scope of the experiment is up the objective end of the objective-subjective continuum. He also realizes that there is no logical contradiction between 'mechanism' descriptions of phenomena and 'meaning' descriptions. He realizes that many levels of description are both valid and necessary.

In fact the Christian scientist has an incentive for his research in the Biblical injunction to 'subdue the earth'. For him, as for Kepler centuries earlier, discovery is but the 'thinking of God's thoughts after him'. Further discovery leads naturally to awe and wonder at the intricacy of God's universe. There is always the realization that the more we seem to discover, the less we seem to know. The knowledge of the universe seems to be as inexhaustible as God himself. This in itself leads to worship.

Science is restored to its rightful place only when the God of the whole universe is made the God of science. It is only then that science itself ceases to be god. When the world's fundamental reference-point is restored, then the main reason for the reaction against science is removed. If there is real ultimate meaning in the universe, then no amount of mechanistic descriptions are going to destroy that meaning. Science ceases to be a threat.

But equally it is not seen as the panacea for all ills. It is recognized that the answers to man's basic problems do not lie within science itself, or the applications of science. No changing of the environment is going to change man himself. The methodology of science may cease to be a threat, but its potential misuses are still as large as ever. Evil is still rampant in the world. Since the Christian holds a realistic view of man's nature, he will hold no naïvely optimistic ideas about the potential uses or misuses of current research. One of the tasks of the Christian community is to infiltrate society in an effort to use science for good rather than for evil purposes.

Scientists themselves often have very little say about how the results of their research are to be used. The decisions are made by industrial boards, or in government departments, or in parliamentary debates. As members of the new community are scattered at every level of society their job is therefore to influence decisions in directions which will be such as to uphold pro-human values, and to use science so that it will be to the maximum benefit of the maximum number of people, rather than increasing the comfort of only a few. The basic command is always the same, to love our neighbour as ourselves. Such influence on society will not be restricted simply to those actually making the decisions, but in influencing public opinion to bring pressure on decision-making bodies.

What scientists do have more specific control over is the direction which their research will take. We have already noted in chapter one the enormous amount of research at present being carried out which appears to have a very high potential for evil and the eventual devaluation of man. Often there is some immediate medical justification in the research which means that it will be continued, even though the negative uses of the findings could be catastrophic. But there is also some research where the positive applications are likely to be very limited, but where the negative results could be very far-reaching. The function of the Christian scientist is to try to direct research into channels where the possibilities for negative applications will at least be no greater than the possibilities for positive application.

That some research topics seem suspect does not mean that research must always be justified by some direct possibility of

positive application. If this were the case, then a very large proportion of scientific research would come to a complete standstill.
In fact very little is carried out with some specific application in
view. It is quite impossible to predict accurately the long-term
results of research without actually doing it. As is well known,
many major discoveries have been made while carrying out
research on something quite different. Nothing could have
directed Alexander Fleming to discover penicillin, because nobody
knew it was there. The disease phenylketonuria was discovered
only because someone noticed a green colour using ferric
chloride when testing the urine of certain mental defectives for
the presence of diabetes. So we could go on: it is of the essence of
a discovery that you do not know what it is until you get there.

At the same time the new community will be concerned to
channel the general directions of research into those things which
are going to alleviate human suffering directly. For example it
seems extraordinary that so much attention and money is being
poured into research on human ageing – particularly when the
average life-expectancy in the west is moving into the sixties and
seventies, and in many countries it is still in the thirties and
forties. When one-third of the world's population suffers from
malnutrition, is it really a priority goal to try to increase the age
of a few privileged people in the west whose age is increasing
anyway due to increased medical care? Should we not be concerned with making living conditions better for the old people
that we already do have, rather than creating even more?

An irrationally distorted view of death can only have the effect
of channelling research money and talent into directions which
are not really restoring man's real humanity. A more valuable
direction might be to spend more research and money on major
diseases such as schizophrenia. Over 500,000 people in Britain
alone suffer from schizophrenia, and it is, after accidents, the
commonest single cause of chronic disabling illness in young
adults. Yet very little is known about its causes, and there is even
little agreement about how it should be defined. Schizophrenia is
diagnosed twice as often in New York as in London among

patients admitted to mental hospitals, but the variation in figures is due to differing methods of diagnosis, rather than to any other factor. Surely the suffering of so many people throughout their lives is more important than adding a few more years onto the lifespan of a small privileged group?

Man has an absolute value because made by an absolute God, so the Christian has a real basis for judgment when it comes to a whole range of ethical questions concerning experiments on human beings, with reference to such things as artificial reproduction and the control of the mind and genetical inheritance. As we noted in chapters one and three, humanistic assumptions fail completely at this point because they give no guide-lines as to what a human being is supposed to be. As Dr C. G. Scorer has pointed out: 'It may be that new human life will be produced artificially without human love or human tears or human laughter. But it may well mean that man as he climbs to higher and higher achievement over himself has so distorted his own humanity that he has ceased to be human.' The humanist can only say that a human being is what is, and there is no more to be said than that. The Christian sees in Jesus Christ a perfect model of humanity beside which any other model must be measured.

The Christian also finds the basis for his ethical judgments in the 'creation ideal'. Even though the image of God in man has been marred by his own selfishness, that image is still recognizable. What God originally made was *very* good, but although it has been so spoilt, it is still so *relatively* good that we can trace an ideal. This does not mean that there are glib answers for every single situation, but it does mean that there is a moral basis upon which answers can be established.

For example in God's creative order he has joined together certain things, and man will only tear them asunder at the cost of certain psychological, social and physical consequences whose long-term effects will be to dehumanize him. For example God has joined sex with marriage, marriage with parenthood, and child-rearing with the home. To pull them apart is wrong because it is in effect calling God a liar in saying that he does not know best for the very human beings that he has created, and because man himself will ultimately suffer by moving further away from God's creation ideal.

Artificial insemination by donor (AID) is therefore a breach of the marriage bond because it means imparting into the relationship something from outside, something which does not stem from the relationship itself. This is wrong in itself because it falls short of the creation ideal, and also because, if practised on a large scale, it will have harmful social and psychological effects; for example many people would be unknowingly half-brothers or half-sisters, and fathers would tend to care less for other people's children. The foundation of sperm banks will have the effect of accelerating this mechanizing tendency by placing increasing emphasis on the quality of the sperm (however that is measured), rather than on the joyful humanity of a marriage relationship. It is only the united sharing of two people that will eventually lead to the emotional link and bond of affection with their offspring which is so essential for the normal development of a child. Already during the past 17 years nearly 400 successful pregnancies have been initiated by researchers with frozen sperm. With sperm banks it will be possible to offer a woman who wants a child a choice of donor, probably including a number of famous or brilliant men whose seed had been contributed or sold to the bank. The fact that there might be a serious danger of the proliferation of recessive genes by such methods does not seem to worry the commercial owners of the two private corporations in America which are already launching such banks. The thought of a woman 'shopping around' for the particular qualities that she would like to see in her offspring hardly encourages one to believe that these trends will lead to a greater humanization of mankind.

Similar arguments apply to hopes that it will eventually be possible to produce children completely artificially in the laboratory, or produce 'clones' of identical children. One would think that only some insanely impersonal military or technocratic power would ever be mad enough to do it, but people have done such mad things in the past that it can never be discounted as a possibility. Clearly the Christian community must fight any attempt to lay such a mechanistic emphasis on man, rather than on his value and meaning as part of a family relationship. It should be made clear that only within the framework of the 'creation ideal' is there a rational basis for such an objection. Opposition on other grounds would have to be based on the dangers of immediate technical difficulties, or on the emotional revulsion which might instinctively be felt at such possibilities. Yet both technical problems and emotional revulsion can be overcome by further research on the one hand, and by persistent propaganda on the other. If there is said to be no real basis for the value of man as he is, this automatically eliminates any rational arguments against manipulating him into something perhaps unrecognizably different.

On the same basis of the creation ideal, the new community would oppose any attempt by a technocratic or totalitarian élite to impose family control systems which would involve genetic engineering. The narrowly biological goals of higher IQ, reproductive capacity, work output and so on, which are the type of genetic goals which scientists sometimes put forward, would be challenged with the more human values of creativity, capacity for relationships, emotional competence and freedom of choice. In fact it is unlikely in the extreme that any genetic manipulation could have clear-cut results on such complex facets of man's humanity. In any event there would always be the major block that it would be impossible to determine the final results of genetic manipulations until many years after they had been performed. The value of the individual in this case would always be upheld.

Similarly attempts to create a man-animal chimaera would be attacked on the basis of the creation ideal because God clearly created man as having a distinct value and position in the universe in contradistinction to the animal kingdom. There is no justification in undoing what God has already done by absorbing animal tissues in such a way that they would have an effect on the nature of man's character and intelligence.

In the area of mind control the Christian emphasis must fall on the right of the individual to have the freedom of choice without restriction by any outside body using violence, drugs or brain-washing techniques. This freedom stems directly from the purposes of God in giving man a real moral choice. But at the same time part of this creation ideal involves a responsibility towards others in society. The freedom of the mind is not an anarchistic freedom. It recognizes the rights of other individuals. There is therefore a limit on what the individual by his own free will can absorb to affect his mind, because what he does with his own mind will inevitably affect other people. If he gets drunk or takes LSD and becomes violent this will affect others. With cannabis the effects may be less noticeable in the short-term, but quite distinct in the long-term. Richard Neville in his book *Playpower* says that 'cannabis teaches us to relax again, drains competitive zeal and encourages laziness – which is going to be important in the future'. The underground magazines have themselves blamed cannabis for the lack of enthusiasm and zeal in the revolution. Those who have been regular cannabis smokers at university tend to be disinclined to settle into any particular career subsequently. In other words the result tends simply to be laziness.

Another effect of 'mind-expanding' drugs is a distortion of the senses, particularly relating to space and time, together with a mild euphoria. Now man as created is placed in a visible world which is a real world, one which is really there because it has been created by a God who is really there. Anything which distorts that reality is therefore in the realm of untruth. The person smoking pot is moving away from truth, not towards truth. He is also involved in denying his own capacity for free choice, because his range of choices becomes reduced by the resultant distortions of reality. Simultaneously, the luxurious sense of laziness means that any real loving, real caring for his neighbour, will be reduced. There is no support for the claim that cannabis helps you to love others, because there is no genuine way of loving another person whom your own senses are interpreting falsely. You are in fact trying to love a distortion of the person, not the real person in the real world. The ultimate effect is once again a denial of humanity rather than a reinforcement of it, because there is a shift away from the real world.

At every level of the attempt to work out the new creation in the present world, there is a rational basis for action because the world is a rational place. We have picked out a few samples to show the far-reaching implications of what happens when the God of the universe is made the God of science. It is only by these means that science and its uses can be restored to something approaching normality. It is only through recognizing the *source* of reason that there comes a block to anti-rationalism and the new mysticism.

The permanent revolution

In the late 1840s Marx propounded the idea of a 'permanent revolution' in his well-known 'Address to the Communist League'. Marxist theorists ever since have battled over what the idea really means, not least Trotsky who wrote a book about it called *The Permanent Revolution*. In essence Marx proposed that there should be no once-and-for-all revolution, but rather a continuing process whereby all social relations would be transformed and a truly communist society established. The mark of this society would be a long-lasting revolution at every level which would change the economy, science and technology, the family, morals and every other aspect of man's life.

This type of revolution as Marx envisaged it has never taken place, nor does it seem remotely likely that it ever will take place. The reason why it has never happened, as we have seen, is that man remains basically the same despite changes in his environment. In the light of this many have become completely cynical about man and his possibilities as they have watched one political idea after another, one social reform after another, founder on the rock of man's own nature. Together with this cynicism about man has come the disaffection with science and the flight from reason.

What then is the way forward? The answer is not to run away from science, nor from reason, nor from man himself, nor to wish all these things away. Nor is there a 'different' world which can be found through drugs or any of the other means used to escape into mysticism. One of the most terrifying things for a person who is becoming mentally ill is the loss of distinction between the real and the unreal. Flight from reason into the unreal is not the way of the future.

Nor are optimistic views of progress which are totally unrelated to real evidence and the real world the kind of answer which is going to show the way forward. An answer that is to satisfy must *both* account for the real world *and* not limit man to what is less than human by removing the physical, or the mental, or the spiritual, or any other aspects of man's social, rational, artistic or moral capabilities.

It is the Christian claim that only in a personal relationship with God is a truly permanent revolution possible. Only as people enter into the new creation is there any hope of permanent change. In this sense the permanent revolution takes place not through the founding of a new political system, nor through some other material change in the environment, but through a day-by-day relationship of individuals with their Creator, who gives them the power to remove the shackles of their own selfishness. The revolution therefore takes place at a personal level, and it is through the infiltration of society by such individuals that society is transformed.

The only way through is the Christian way. Christian theism, the fact that God has created and sustained the universe, and that he has spoken in verifiable history, keeps man firmly based in the real physical world. Jesus really came, and died, and was raised to life again. His physical body before the resurrection was limited by space and time in the same way as any other physical body. His teaching was firmly implanted in the world of things. His promises of forgiveness for sin and new life can be tried and tested, and today many are turning to him as their source of real life and permanent change.

The Christian way does not limit man to the methods and restrictions of science and history. Man is not just allowed to be human, rather he is positively given the only means whereby his lost humanity can be restored. The new creation, now co-existent with the old, can begin to show already what the world should really be like – and what in the new heavens and new earth, it will be like. For God will have the last word.

BIBLIOGRAPHY

A list of books referred to or quoted from in the text

ANDERSON, J. N. D., *Christianity and Comparative Religion*, Tyndale Press, 1970.

AYER, A. J., *Language, Truth and Logic*, Gollancz, 1946.

BECKETT, Samuel, *Malone Dies*, Calder and Boyars, 1968.

BLACKHAM, H. J. (Ed.), *Objections to Humanism*, Constable, 1963.

BLACKHAM, H. J., *Humanism*, Penguin, 1968.

BRONOWSKI, J., *The Common Sense of Science*, Heinemann, 1961 and Penguin, 1968.

BRONOWSKI, J., *The Identity of Man*, Heinemann, 1965 and Penguin, 1967.

BROW, Robert, *Religion: Origins and Ideas*, Tyndale Press, 1966.

BROWN, Colin, *Philosophy and the Christian Faith*, Tyndale Press, 1969.

BRUCE, F. F., *The New Testament Documents*, Inter-Varsity Press, 1960.

BRYANT, John, *Health and the Developing World*, Cornell University Press, 1971.

BUTTERFIELD, H., *The Origins of Modern Science*, Bell, 1962.

CAHN, S. M., *Fate, Logic and Time*, Yale University Press, 1967.

CALDER, Nigel, *The Mind of Man*, BBC Publications, 1971.

CALDER, Ritchie, *Man and the Cosmos*, Pall Mall Press, 1968.

CAMUS, Albert, *The Outsider*, Hamish Hamilton, 1946.

CAMUS, Albert, *The Rebel*, Hamish Hamilton, 1953.

CAMUS, Albert, *The Myth of Sisyphus*, Hamish Hamilton, 1955.

CAMUS, Albert, *The Fall*, Hamish Hamilton, 1957.

CLARK, G. H., *The Philosophy of Science and Belief in God*, Craig Press, 1964.

CLARK, R. E. D., *Christian Belief and Science*, Fortress, 1961.

CLARKE, Robin, *The Science of War and Peace*, Jonathan Cape.

COCKBURN, A. and BLACKBURN, R., *Student Power*, Penguin, 1969.

COHN-BENDIT, G. and D., *Obsolete Communism: The Left-Wing Alternative*, Penguin, 1969.

CULLMANN, O., *Immortality of the Soul or Resurrection of the Dead*, Epworth, 1958.

DARLINGTON, C. D., *The Evolution of Man and Society*, Allen and Unwin, 1969.

DARWIN, Charles, *The Origin of Species*, available from Penguin, 1970.

EHRLICH, Paul, *The Population Bomb*, Ballantine Books, 1971.

EHRLICH, Paul and HARRIMAN, R. L., *How to be a Survivor: A Plan to Save Spaceship Earth*, Ballantine Books, 1971.

ELLUL, Jacques, *The Technological Society*, Cape, 1965.

EVANS-PRITCHARD, E. E., *Theories of Primitive Religion*, Oxford University Press, 1965.

EYSENCK, H. J., *Race, Intelligence and Education*, Temple-Smith, 1971.

FLEW, Anthony, *Evolutionary Ethics*, Macmillan, 1968.

FLEW, Anthony, *God and Philosophy*, Hutchinson, 1966.

FRAZER, George, *The Golden Bough*, Macmillan, 1936.

FREUD, Sigmund, *Totem and Taboo*, Routledge and Kegan Paul, 1950.

FREUD, Sigmund, *The Future of an Illusion*, Doubleday, 1925.

FUCHS, Stephen, *The Origin of Man and his Culture*, Asia Publishing House, 1963.

GREEN, Michael, *Man Alive!*, Inter-Varsity Press, 1967.

GRUNBERGER, Richard, *A Social History of the Third Reich*, Weidenfeld and Nicholson, 1971.

HAMILTON, Alistair, *The Appeal of Fascism*, Macmillan, 1970.

HANNENA, Sjoerd, *Fads, Fakes and Fantasies*, Macdonald, 1970.

HOYLE, Sir Fred, *The Nature of the Universe*, Penguin, 1960.

HUME, David, *An Enquiry Concerning Human Understanding*, Oxford University Press, 1961.

HUXLEY, Aldous, *Brave New World*, available from Penguin, 1969.

HUXLEY, Aldous, *The Doors of Perception*, Chatto and Windus, 1954.

HUXLEY, Julian (Ed.), *The Humanist Frame*, Allen and Unwin, 1961.

HUXLEY, Julian, *The Essays of a Humanist*, Penguin, 1966.

HUXLEY, Julian, *Evolutionary Ethics*, Pilot Press.

JACKMAN, Stuart, *The Davidson Affair*, Faber, 1968.

JEEVES, Malcolm, *The Scientific Enterprise and Christian Faith*, Tyndale Press, 1969.

JEVENS, F. B., *Introduction to the History of Religion*, London, 1896.

KESEY, Kenneth, *One Flew over the Cuckoo's Nest*, Viking, 1964.

KING-HELE, Desmond, *The End of the Twentieth Century*, St Martin, 1970.

KOESTLER, Arthur, *The Ghost in the Machine*, Hutchinson, 1967.

KUEZLI, Arnold, *Karl Marx: Eine Psychographie*, Europa-Verlag, 1966.

LANCELOT, Michel, *Je Veux Regarder Dieu en Face*, Albin-Michel, 1970.

LENIN, N., *The State and Revolution* (from Selected Works, Vol. 2), Lawrence and Wishard, 1964.

LEWIS, H. D. and SLATER, R. L., *World Religions*, C. A. Watts, 1966.

LEWIS, C. S., *Out of the Silent Planet*, Longman, 1966 and Pan, 1968.

LORENZ, Konrad, *On Aggression*, Methuen, 1966.

MACKAY, D. M., *Freedom of Action in a Mechanistic Universe*, Cambridge University Press, 1967.

MACKAY, D. M., in *Brain and Conscious Experience*, ed. Sir John Eccles, Pontifica Accademia della Scienze, Springer-Verlag, 1966.

MACKAY, D. M. (Ed.), *Christianity in a Mechanistic Universe*, Inter-Varsity Press, 1965.

MCLUHAN, Marshall, in *Understanding Media: The Extensions of Man*, ed. Edmund Carpenter, Sphere Books, 1970.

MCLUHAN, Marshall, *Explorations in Communication*, Beacon Press, 1960.

MANVELL, Roger and FRAENKL, Heinrich, *The Incomparable Crime*, Putnam, 1967.

MARX, Karl, *Capital*, various edns., e.g. Lawrence and Ward, 1970.

MARX, Karl and ENGELS, Friedrich, *The German Ideology*, Lawrence and Ward, 1970.

MEDAWAR, Sir Peter, *The Art of the Soluble*, Methuen, 1967 and Penguin, 1969.

MERTON, R. K., *Social Theory and Social Structure*, Free Press, New York, 1957.

MILLS, C. W., *The Marxists*, Penguin, 1963.

MONOD, Jacques, *Chance and Necessity*, Collins, 1972.

MORRIS, Desmond, *The Naked Ape*, Jonathan Cape, 1967.

MORRIS, Desmond, *The Human Zoo*, Jonathan Cape, 1969.

NAGLOVSKY, Alexander, 'Reminiscences' in *Sovremennyya Zapiski*, Paris, No. 61.

NEVILLE, Richard, *Playpower*, Jonathan Cape, 1970 and Paladin, 1971.

NIETZSCHE, F., *Thus Spoke Zarathustra*, Penguin, 1969.

ODAJNYK, Walter, *Marxism and Existentialism*, Doubleday, 1965.

ORWELL, George, *Nineteen Eighty-Four*, Penguin, 1954.

PAUL, Leslie, *Alternatives to Christian Belief*, Hodder and Stoughton, 1967.

POLANYI, Michael, *Knowing and Being*, Routledge and Kegan Paul, 1969.

REICH, Charles, *The Greening of America*, Random House, 1970.

ROOKMAAKER, H. R., *Modern Art and the Death of a Culture*, Inter-Varsity Press, 1970.

ROSZAK, Theodore, *The Making of a Counter Culture*, Faber, 1970.

RUSSELL, Bertrand, *Autobiography*, Vol. 3, Allen and Unwin, 1967.

SARRAUTE, Nathalie, *The Golden Fruits*, Calder and Boyars, 1967.

SARTRE, Jean-Paul, *Existentialism and Humanism*, Methuen, 1948.

SCHAEFFER, Francis, *Escape from Reason*, Inter-Varsity Press, 1968.

SCHAEFFER, Francis, *Pollution and the Death of Man*, Hodder and Stoughton, 1970.

SCHMIDT, W., *The Origin and Growth of Religion*, Methuen, 1931.

SEALE, P. and MCCONVILLE, M., *French Revolution 1968*, Penguin, 1968.

SHUB, David, *Lenin*, Doubleday, 1948.

SKINNER, B. F., *Walden Two*, Collier-Macmillan, 1962.

STORR, Anthony, *Christian Essays in Psychology.*

TAYLOR, G. R., *The Biological Time-Bomb*, Thames and Hudson, 1968.

TEILHARD DE CHARDIN, M.-J.-P., *The Phenomenon of Man*, Collins, 1959.

TINSLEY, E. J., 'Mysticism' in *A Dictionary of Christian Theology*, ed. Alan Richardson, SCM Press, 1969.

TROTSKY, Leon, *The Revolution Betrayed*, New Park, 1967.

TROTSKY, Leon, *The Permanent Revolution*, Pioneer Publishers, 1931.

TSE-TUNG, Mao, *On the General Handling of Contradictions among the People*, New Century Publishers, 1957.

WATSON, J. D., *The Double Helix*, Weidenfeld and Nicolson, 1968.

WALTER, W. G., *The Living Brain*, Penguin, 1968.

WELLS, H. G., *The Mind at the End of Its Tether.*

WURMBRAND, R., *Tortured for Christ*, Hodder and Stoughton, 1967.

INDEX